NASSAU BOULEVARD
GARDEN CITY ESTATES

GARDEN CITY, LONG ISLAND
in Early Photographs, 1869–1919

by M. H. SMITH
with the assistance of Jeanmarie DiNoto

DOVER PUBLICATIONS, INC.
New York

ACKNOWLEDGMENTS

This pictorial history of Garden City's first fifty years is almost entirely composed of early photographs from the village's extensive archive collection housed in the Garden City Public Library. The collection is based primarily on original photographs donated by George Loring Hubbell, resident manager of the Garden City Company and Garden City's first mayor, and by Anne Townsend McKellar, one of the village's earliest residents. Other longtime residents have contributed important photographs to the archives as well, including the Stewart wedding portraits (from Louise Osborne Longmore), two 1877 glass-plate prints of the Cathedral of the Incarnation (from Rev. Harold F. Lemoin), the panorama of Garden City (from Robert D. Harrower), the Hazelhurst Field photographs (from Gerard Hughes) and the view of Camp Mills (from Mrs. Charles E. Clark). Credit has been given in the captions for photographs obtained from sources other than the Garden City archives. Vincent Seyfried, Long Island historian and author, has assisted by checking the original prints and having reproductions made when necessary.

The historical content of the captions is largely based on my *History of Garden City*, the village's official history, recently republished in an updated edition by the Garden City Historical Society. Its sources are listed in its bibliography, which has been augmented for this volume.

Jeanmarie DiNoto, a founder and current president of the Garden City Historical Society, has assisted me from the first in planning the format of this book, in presenting the plan to the village and the publisher and in choosing the most appropriate illustrations.

Publication of the present volume has been made possible by the support of the Incorporated Village of Garden City, the cooperation of the Garden City Historical Society and the Garden City Public Library, and the advice and personal interest of Hayward Cirker, president of Dover Publications.

Copyright © 1987 by Garden City Historical Society.
All rights reserved under Pan American and International Copyright Conventions.

Published in Canada by General Publishing Company, Ltd., 30 Lesmill Road, Don Mills, Toronto, Ontario.
Published in the United Kingdom by Constable and Company, Ltd., 10 Orange Street, London WC2H 7EG.

Garden City, Long Island, in Early Photographs, 1869–1919 is a new work, first published by Dover Publications, Inc., in 1987.

Manufactured in the United States of America
Dover Publications, Inc., 31 East 2nd Street, Mineola, N.Y. 11501

Book design by Carol Belanger Grafton

Library of Congress Cataloging-in-Publication Data

Smith, M. H. (Mildred Hess), 1901–
  Garden City, Long Island in early photographs, 1869–1919.

  Bibliography: p.
  Includes index.
  1. Garden City (N.Y.)—History—Pictorial works. 2. Garden City (N.Y.)—Description—Views. I. DiNoto, Jeanmarie. II. Title.
  F129.G15S49   1987   974.7′245   87-17115
  ISBN 0-486-25556-5 (pbk.)

A BRIEF HISTORY OF GARDEN CITY

The news on July 17, 1869, that the multimillionaire "merchant prince" Alexander Turney Stewart had purchased over 7,000 acres of the Hempstead Plains on Long Island came as a shock to the New York business world. The size of the tract and the $395,328 paid in cash made it the biggest private land purchase of the century. Equally surprising were the unpromising location of this flat interior tract of land and Stewart's promise to the Township of Hempstead "to spend from six to ten millions of dollars to develop it for actual settlers."

Formed during the Ice Age from glacial outwash, the Hempstead Plains had become a natural prairie with only enough accumulated soil to support, as Daniel Denton wrote in 1670, "very fine grass that makes exceeding good Hay and very good pasture for sheep and other cattel." The Plains had been used for this purpose from Denton's time until the nineteenth century, when the livestock industry moved to the Western prairies. By 1869 it had become a neglected and treeless wasteland.

Undaunted by the obvious problems involved, A. T. Stewart, with his architect, John Kellum, spent the rest of that year planning and mapping the village he had decided to build between Mineola on the north and Hempstead on the south. Since much of the work was done in Kellum's office, it can be said that Garden City had its beginnings on a drawing board. Stewart's new Central Railroad of Long Island, which would provide transportation to the village and the plainland beyond, was to run straight through the center of the village. A grid pattern of avenues and streets was then carefully delineated; a centrally located 23-acre park was set aside for a grand hotel; a stable and carriage house and store blocks were placed near the railroad; an all-important waterworks was located to the north; and eighty-odd houses were assigned to avenues and streets according to size, importance and convenience. Within seven years this planned village, one of the first of its kind in America, had been transferred from the blueprints to the chosen ploughed and graded site. To complete the village, Stewart had thousands of trees brought in from nurseries in Flushing and Jamaica to line the wide avenues and streets and to landscape the hotel park, the station plaza and the grounds of all the residences. This planting, which was to be continually improved over the years, was one of the most important aspects of Stewart's plans for the village he had named Garden City.

The early photographs in this book show how lavishly and optimistically Stewart carried out his plans. Everything is on a generous scale—the unusually wide avenues and streets, the handsome four-story hotel, the impressive row of stores, the tall, elegant houses and the castlelike waterworks, which included the largest well on Long Island. But we also see how bare and empty the new village must have been during those first few years. We look in vain for a stableboy or groom at the door of the big stable and carriage house, for a group of guests arriving at the hotel or railroad station, for a nursemaid and child in a garden. It is actually a relief to see the butcher in his apron at the door of his shop, an admiring group posing with one of Stewart's new steam locomotives and some neatly tied-back curtains in the windows of a house on Hilton Avenue.

Very few settlers had come to live in Garden City by the time Stewart died in 1876. This was partly because the houses were not available for sale; they were rented on an annual basis from the Stewart Estate, which made all necessary repairs and maintained the grounds. The character of the village was to change dramatically, however, when his widow, Cornelia Clinch Stewart, decided to honor his memory by building a large Gothic cathedral, a bishop's residence and two Cathedral schools, and deeding the land and buildings to the Episcopal Diocese of Long Island in perpetuity. It was an enduring gift to Garden City as well, giving it purpose, stability and prestige.

Seven years after Mrs. Stewart's death in 1886, her more worldly heirs added a new dimension to Garden City by forming the Garden City Company to develop its recreational and social potential. The famous firm of McKim, Mead & White was called in to transform the Victorian hotel into a beautiful Georgian building; the famous Garden City Golf Course was built; the recreational Casino was remodeled; an elite gun club was welcomed; and polo at Meadow Brook was encouraged and patronized. Of even more importance, the Estate system was abolished and the land and houses were placed on the market, under farsighted restrictions. During the next decade, the Garden City Company built several model homes in the style then popular and sold them to new settlers. All these improvements launched Garden City into the role of a popular, exclusive resort for the sportsminded and wealthy of New York, Brooklyn and Long Island.

At the turn of the century, Garden City became part of newly created Nassau County, with the new County Court House within its borders on Franklin Avenue. The firm of McKim, Mead & White was rebuilding the fire-damaged hotel into a larger and even more attractive one. And a new railroad station was welcoming an ever-increasing number of guests and visitors. The horse and carriage was still a common sight, but the automobile had arrived with wealthy sportsman William K. Vanderbilt, Jr., who organized the exciting Vanderbilt Cup Races, using the hotel as headquarters. The very flatness and treelessness of the Hempstead Plains now made it a desirable place for automobile roadracing, the development of a motor parkway and an entirely new and dramatic sport—aviation. Two small airports in the northern section of Garden City were soon attracting pioneer aviators, inventors and experimenters—and crowds. Quite unexpectedly, Garden City and the Hempstead Plains had become the "Cradle of Aviation."

In 1907 the time had come for a new phase of development— Garden City was to become a suburb. The Long Island Railroad was already electrifying the Hempstead Branch (Stewart's

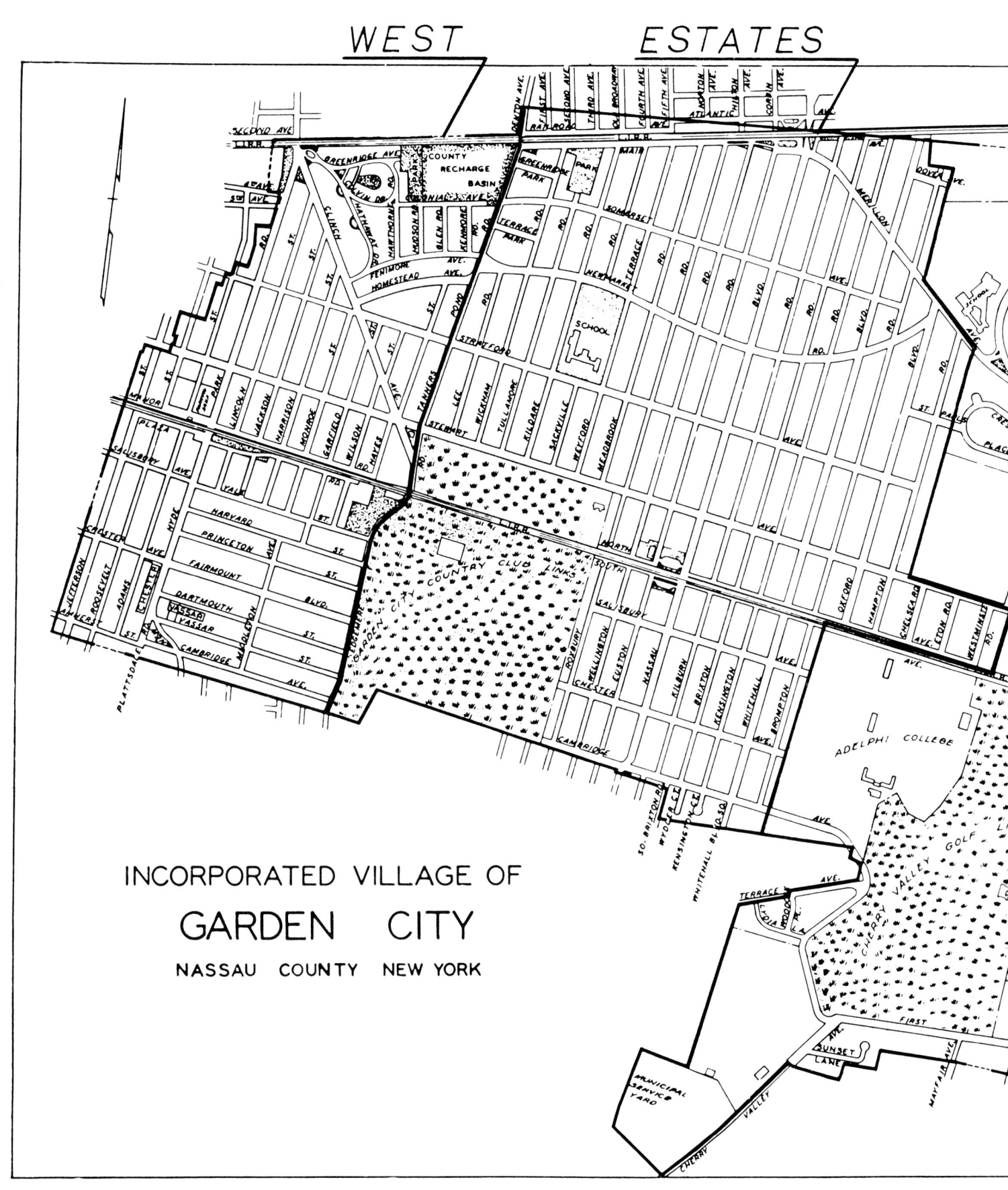

Official map of Garden City.

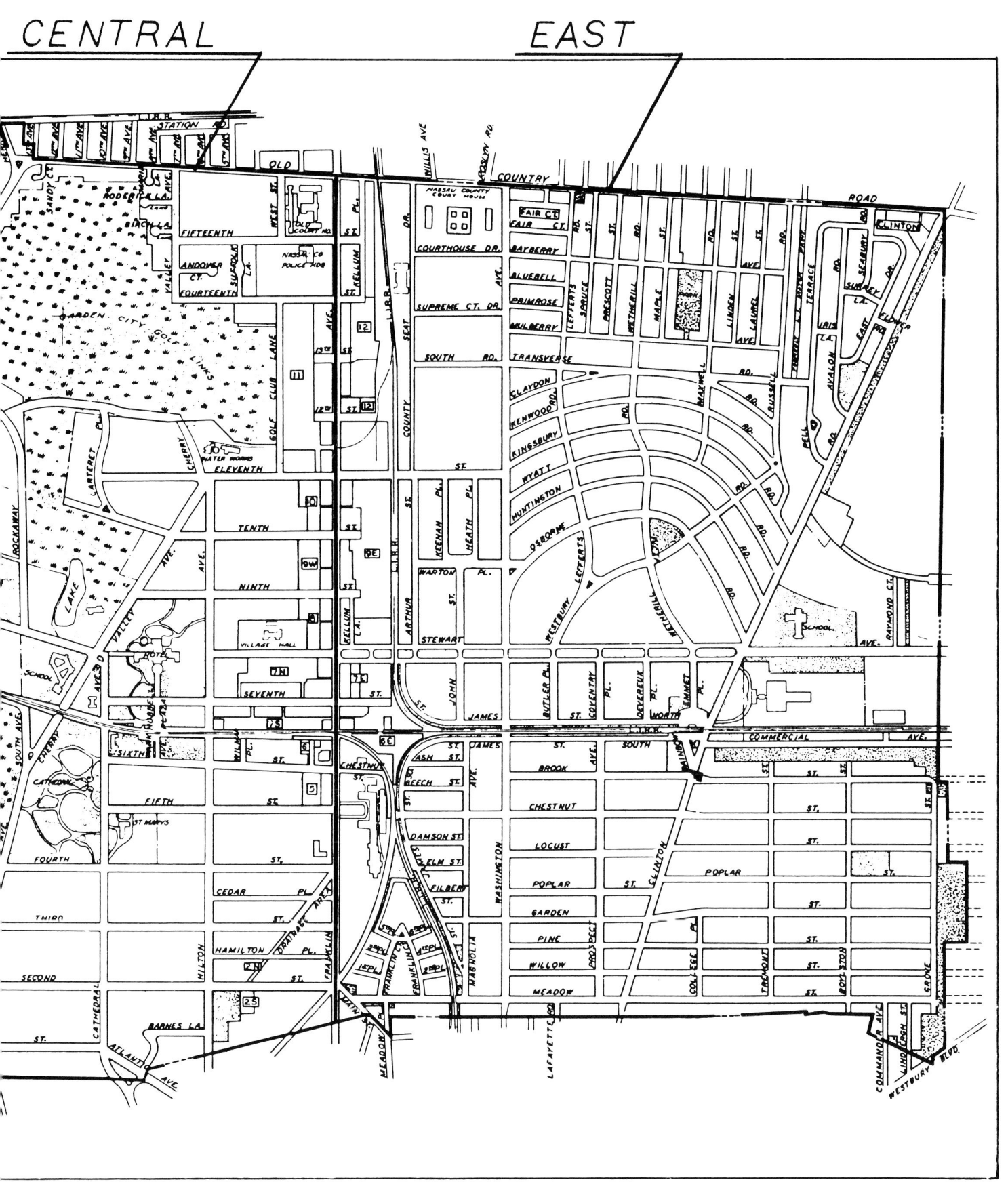

Central Railroad) and would soon complete the tunnel connection to Pennsylvania Station in New York. With such assured transportation, suburban growth on Long Island was inevitable. That year a group of wealthy businessmen in New York formed a corporation, bought a square mile of land west of central Garden City from the Garden City Company and developed the community of Garden City Estates. Very like Garden City in planning and execution, it became so successful that the Garden City Company decided to develop the eastern section of the village as well.

By 1910 the Company's plans for this section were completed. It lay to the east of "Old Garden City" and extended from Franklin Avenue to Clinton Road, where a railroad station was soon built on the Central Railroad. Called "Subdivision East," its main feature was Stewart Avenue, which consisted of a dual highway planted with six rows of trees, enclosing a parklike mall. Impressive in width and design, it became an avenue of large and handsome houses. It also became a link between the Garden City Hotel and the entrance to the Long Island Motor Parkway, which William K. Vanderbilt was building from Garden City to Lake Ronkonkoma for automobile enthusiasts. Franklin Avenue itself, with its convenient trolley, inevitably became Garden City's main thoroughfare. It had already been chosen in 1910 as the new address of the publishing house of Doubleday, Page & Company, which was setting a trend by moving its publishing house from New York City to a suburb. In 1912, Garden City East also acquired the Hempstead Plains Aerodrome on Clinton Road north of the Motor Parkway—a sophisticated, well-equipped airfield built to replace Garden City's two smaller ones, which had become obstacles to suburban growth.

Five years later, when the United States entered World War I in 1917, this airfield, renamed Hazelhurst Field, was taken over by the government to train Army pilots. Other military installations on Clinton Road soon followed, and the Curtiss Engineering plant was built north of the railroad tracks to develop four Navy antisubmarine hydroplanes. Just south of the tracks, the Army took over the large southeast corner of Garden City to establish Camp Mills for the purpose of mobilizing the Rainbow Division. By the end of the year, all the land east of Clinton Road in Garden City was being used in the war effort, and the Central Railroad was playing an indispensable role in transporting troops (secretly at night), prefabricated parts to the Curtiss plant, and an endless flow of supplies to Camp Mills.

By the end of the war, the three sections of Garden City covered almost all of the 5.2 square miles of Stewart's original master plan, and were faced with new challenges and responsibilities. Unwilling to be governed any longer by two private corporations, the residents of the three sections—Garden City Estates, Old Garden City and Garden City East—decided to unite and incorporate under an unusual, nonpolitical form of government called the Community (or Gentlemen's) Agreement, with each section represented on a board of trustees. On May 15, 1919, at the end of those first exciting fifty years, Mr. Stewart's "planned village" became the Incorporated Village of Garden City, Hempstead Town, Common School District No. 18 (population 2,140). (In 1931, Garden City West became the fourth section of the village to be represented on the board of trustees.)

Under citizens' control, Garden City was to grow and flourish as a predominantly residential suburban community, guided by A. T. Stewart's high standards and protected by strict zoning and continued planning. By 1987 it was almost at its growth capacity, having an estimated population of 22,927 and about 6,500 homes. Most of the growth has occurred since World War II; the last forty years have witnessed the building of hundreds of smaller, well-designed houses, a restricted number of new apartments, new churches, a medical center, a pool complex and scattered playgrounds. On the two business avenues, high-quality shopping areas have developed, due largely to innovative public parking facilities and firm restrictions. Brokerage houses and insurance companies have been attracted as well. The village's public-school system has been outstanding for many years and has kept pace with the growing population. Higher education is locally available at Adelphi University in Garden City itself and at Hofstra University nearby.

Throughout its business and residential areas, the village has maintained that landscaped neatness and immaculate grooming that make it unusual. It has constantly added to the planting and beautification of its public areas, so that, in spite of growth and change, it remains a true garden city. It is a living tribute to its founder, who has taken his place in history not only as one of the greatest merchants of the nineteenth century but as a city planner of importance.

CONTENTS

MR. AND MRS. ALEXANDER TURNEY STEWART
(pages 1–4)

1. The Stewart Wedding Miniatures
2. Alexander Turney Stewart, 1801–1876
3. The "Great Iron Store"
4. The "Marble Palace"
5, 6. The Stewart Art Collection

PURCHASE OF THE HEMPSTEAD PLAINS
(pages 5–8)

7. The Hempstead Plains
8. The Birdfoot Violet
9. The Stewart Purchase
10. John Kellum, 1809–1871
11. Garden City Master Plan

THE PLANNED VILLAGE
(pages 9–21)

12. The First House
13. James H. L'Hommedieu
14. The Grand Hotel, 1874
15. The Stable and Carriage House, 1874
16. A "Whisky Gig," 1880
17. The Garden City Station, c. 1873
18. A Central Railroad Locomotive
19. The Newtown No. 6
20. The Estate Building, c. 1875
21. An "Apostle" House, 1877
22. A Brick "Disciple" House, c. 1875
23–26. The Smaller Houses
27. The First Stores
28. The Second Store Block
29. A Grammar School Class, c. 1889
30. Workmen's Cottages, 1872
31. The Waterworks, 1876
32. Panorama of Garden City, 1878

THE MEMORIAL CATHEDRAL
(pages 22–30)

33. Cornelia Clinch Stewart, 1803–1886
34. Cathedral Cornerstone Laying
35. The Cathedral of the Incarnation
36. Cathedral Interior
37. The Crypt
38. The Bishop's Residence
39. Laying the Cornerstone of St. Paul's School, 1879
40. Military Exercises, St. Paul's School, 1884
41. St. Paul's Football Team
42. The Cathedral School of St. Mary
43. Consecration of the Cathedral
44. View of the Village, c. 1878

THE GARDEN CITY COMPANY
(pages 31–42)

45. The Stewart Heirs
46. Garden City, 1888
47. The Fairgrounds, c. 1890
48. The Meadow Brook Hunt Club
49. Stanford White, 1853–1906
50. The Remodeled Hotel, c. 1895
51, 52. The Hotel Interior, 1897
53. The Casino, c. 1905
54. Home of George Loring Hubbell
55. The Garden City Golf Club
56. Walter J. Travis
57. The Garden City Gun Club, c. 1894
58. The Carteret Gun Club, c. 1897
59. Lake Cornelia/Hubbell's Pond
60. The Garden City Station, c. 1898
61. A Canopy-Top Surrey
62. The Hotel Fire, 1899

THE TURN OF THE CENTURY
(pages 43–54)

63. The Nassau County Court House
64. Laying the Cornerstone of the County Court House, 1900
65. The Trolley
66. The Restored Hotel
67. The Hotel Porches, 1905
68. Cab Service, 1907
69. The Garden City Garage
70. William K. Vanderbilt, Jr.
71. Vanderbilt Cup Race, 1906
72. Vanderbilt Cup Race, 1908
73. The Gold Bug Hotel, 1909
74. Glenn Hammond Curtiss, 1909
75. The Washington Avenue Airfield, 1909
76. The First Public-School Building
77. A "Little School" Classroom, c. 1905
78. The Firehouse, 1909
79. The Salisbury Links Clubhouse, 1907

GARDEN CITY ESTATES
(pages 55–61)

80. Garden City Estates, 1907
81. Building Nassau Boulevard, 1906
82. The Gage Tarbell House
83. Garden City Estates Station and Plaza, 1908
84. The Estates Clubhouse, 1908
85. The Stable-Garage, 1908
86. The Electric Train, 1908
87. The Garden City Country Club, 1916
88. The Timothy Woodruff House on Stewart Avenue, 1908

89. International Aviation Meet Pennant, 1911
90. Postmaster General Hitchcock and Earle Ovington, 1911
91. The First Airmail Flight, Sept. 23, 1911

GARDEN CITY EAST
(pages 62–71)

92. The Garden City Company Office, 1912
93. Subdivision East, Stewart Avenue
94. The Clinton Road Station, c. 1910
95. The Long Island Motor Parkway
96. The Tollhouse, 1911
97. L. I. Motor Parkway Office
98. Doubleday, Page and Company, 1910
99. Laying the Doubleday Cornerstone, 1910
100. Steam Train at Doubleday Plant
101. Franklin Court, 1912
102. 821 Franklin Avenue, 1910
103. St. Joseph's Church
104. The Hempstead Plains Aerodrome, c. 1912
105. The Moisant Aviation School, 1912
106. An Aviator, 1913

WORLD WAR I
(pages 72–79)

107. Hazelhurst's First Reserve Aero Squadron, 1917
108. Hazelhurst Field, 1917
109. Quentin Roosevelt, c. 1917
110. Camp Mills, 1917
111. The Rainbow Division Monument
112. Entrance to Camp Mills, 1918
113. Lieut. William Bradford Turner
114. The Curtiss Engineering Plant, 1917
115. The NC-4 That Crossed the Atlantic
116. Curtiss Aeroplane and Motor Corp. Interior, 1919
117. British Dirigible, 1919
118. The Village Hall

BIBLIOGRAPHY
(page 81)

INDEX
(page 82)

GARDEN CITY, LONG ISLAND
in Early Photographs, 1869–1919

MR. AND MRS. ALEXANDER TURNEY STEWART

1. The Stewart Wedding Miniatures. Cornelia Mitchell Clinch and Alexander Turney Stewart were married on October 16, 1823. Many young couples were married on that day, and many of those from well-to-do families had their portraits painted. But perhaps none were to leave so large and tangible a legacy as the Stewarts, who were to plan, build and develop the village of Garden City, Long Island.

2. Alexander Turney Stewart, 1801–1876. This portrait of Alexander Turney Stewart was painted by T. P. Rossiter in 1860, when the "merchant prince" was at the height of his career and one of the three richest men in the United States. Of modest Scottish ancestry, Stewart was born after his father's death on a farm near Lisburn, Northern Ireland, in 1801 and raised by his maternal grandfather, John Torney, after his mother remarried and emigrated to America. Although he received a classical education in English secondary academies in Lisburn and Belfast and taught school during a brief visit to the New World, he chose to claim a $10,000 inheritance and become a merchant in New York. His career as a highly inventive and greatly successful merchant is well known—from his start in a small rented wooden building on lower Broadway in 1823 to his ownership of the famous "Great Iron Store." Over the years, Stewart invested heavily in New York real estate—hotels, theaters and rows of brownstone residences; in Saratoga he built the Grand Union Hotel. A staunch advocate of the Union during the Civil War, he filled Army and Navy contracts. He was so helpful in the nomination of U. S. Grant for the presidency that he was offered the post of Secretary of the Treasury (he was not confirmed). Sharing in everything was his wife, Cornelia, daughter of a well-to-do ship chandler. The marriage remained childless after the loss of two children in infancy. They lived in successively larger brownstone houses in New York, summered at Saratoga and traveled to Europe for business and to collect paintings. In 1868 they were ready to move into their own home—the "Marble Palace" on Fifth Avenue.

3. The "Great Iron Store." Wealthier than ever and anticipating the uptown movement of commerce in Manhattan, Stewart built his "Great Iron Store," the largest retail store in the world, in 1862. Located on an entire square block bounded by 9th and 10th Streets, Broadway and Fourth Avenue, it rose five stories above ground, as high as the spire of Grace Church nearby. Two full basement floors provided some of the eighteen acres of selling space that kept the 2,000 employees at work. Famous not only for its size and cost ($2,750,000), it was also one of the first commercial buildings to use an internal iron framework as well as cast-iron walls on all four façades. This exterior use of iron was achieved by fastening uniform precast-iron window panels with slender columns, piers and arches along every floor. Once completed, the entire building was painted a soft "marble" white—from all accounts rather convincing. Inside, the central saloon rose floor by floor, with frescoed walls and ceilings supported by Corinthian iron columns. To right and left were tempting salons displaying satin opera coats lined with fur, cashmere shawls, street wraps, hats, men's furnishings, carpets, artworks, Alexandre gloves and children's wear—in fact, a "departmental" retail store with varied merchandise under one roof. The store was an instant success, and a monument to Mr. Stewart's great reputation as a merchant. It was sold thirty years after his death to Wanamaker's department-store firm.

4. The "Marble Palace." Among the palatial mansions being built on Fifth Avenue, Stewart's "Marble Palace" was notable not only for its size and Italian Renaissance style but because its entire exterior was sheathed in polished Tuckahoe marble. Equally impressive was the interior lined in Carrara marble ordered from Italy. Designed by John Kellum and completed in 1869 at a cost of $1,500,000, the mansion stood on the northwest corner of Fifth Avenue and 34th Street, three stories in height and crowned with a 19-foot mansard roof. Inside, the rooms were immense—the parlor 46 feet long with a 28-foot ceiling, the dining room 19 feet by 32 feet. But there was little social life during the first few years, while Stewart was founding his village of Garden City and pursuing his business interests abroad. A frail man, he became suddenly ill and died in his New York mansion on April 10, 1876. The funeral procession from 34th Street to St.-Mark's-in-The-Bowery was impressive, with flags at half-staff and crowds lining the streets as the 150 carriages passed by. Mrs. Stewart lived on in the lonely residence for the next ten years, spending much of her time in Garden City building a cathedral and two affiliated schools. After her death in 1886, the house was leased to the Manhattan Club and later sold to a syndicate and demolished. This was the end, as one newspaper reported, "of the most costly and luxurious private residence on the Continent."

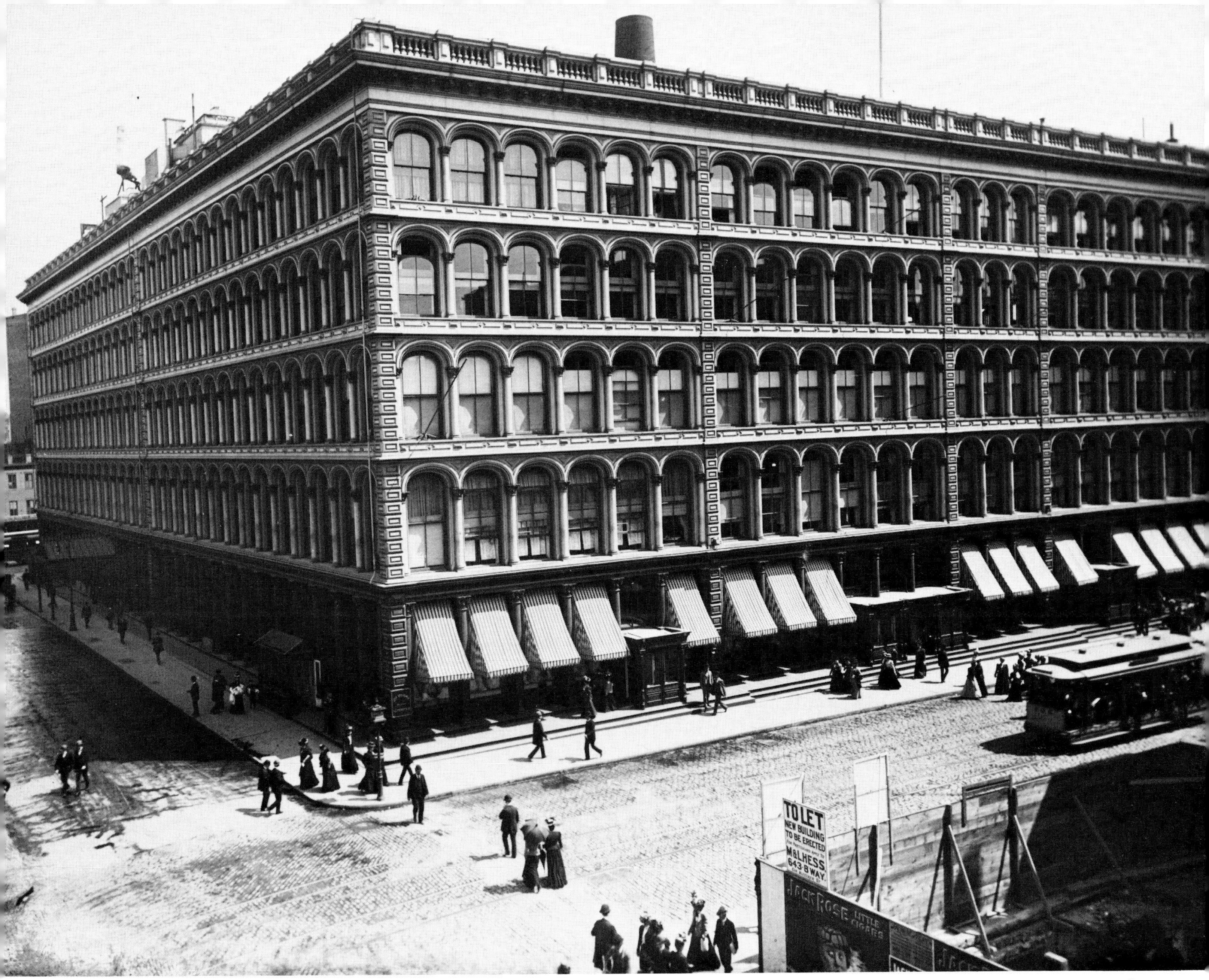
TO LET
NEW BUILDING
TO BE ERECTED
M&L HESS
643 B'WAY
JACK ROSE
LITTLE CIGARS

3

4

3

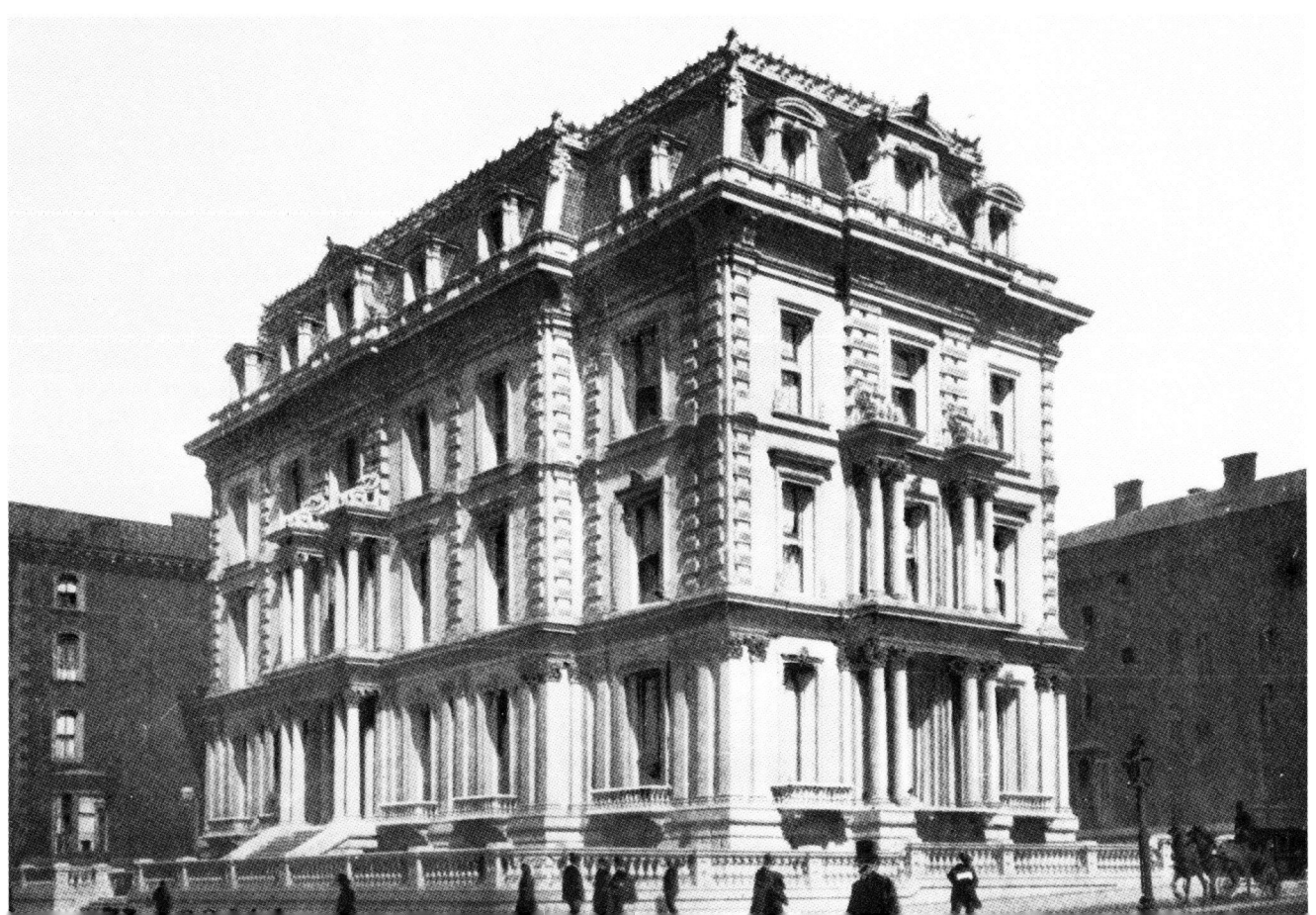

5, 6. The Stewart Art Collection. Looking more like a museum than a home, Stewart's "Marble Palace" was designed to display the large art collection he and his wife had assembled over the years on business trips to Europe. Even the entrance foyer (above), formidable with its elaborately carved Corinthian columns, housed several large pieces of sculpture, which were reflected in wall mirrors. Beyond was the hall and staircase, with *Nydia*, a favorite acquisition, nearby (to the right of the gallery entrance in illustration no. 5). Through the wide, framed doorway one catches a glimpse of the 30′ × 72′ picture gallery—an immense room displaying 200-odd canvases, which covered the walls from floor to ceiling, including Rosa Bonheur's *Horse Fair* (on the far wall in no. 6). Throughout the parlors, bronzes, ceramics and porcelains were on display as well. In 1869, his art collection now in place, Stewart was ready to devote his energies and great wealth to some new project. Almost by chance, in July of that year, his architect, John Kellum, gave him the news that a great tract of land on Long Island, the Hempstead Plains, was for sale. (The collection, reflecting almost entirely the Victorian taste of the nineteenth century, was auctioned after Mrs. Stewart's death and yielded far less than expected.)

PURCHASE OF THE HEMPSTEAD PLAINS

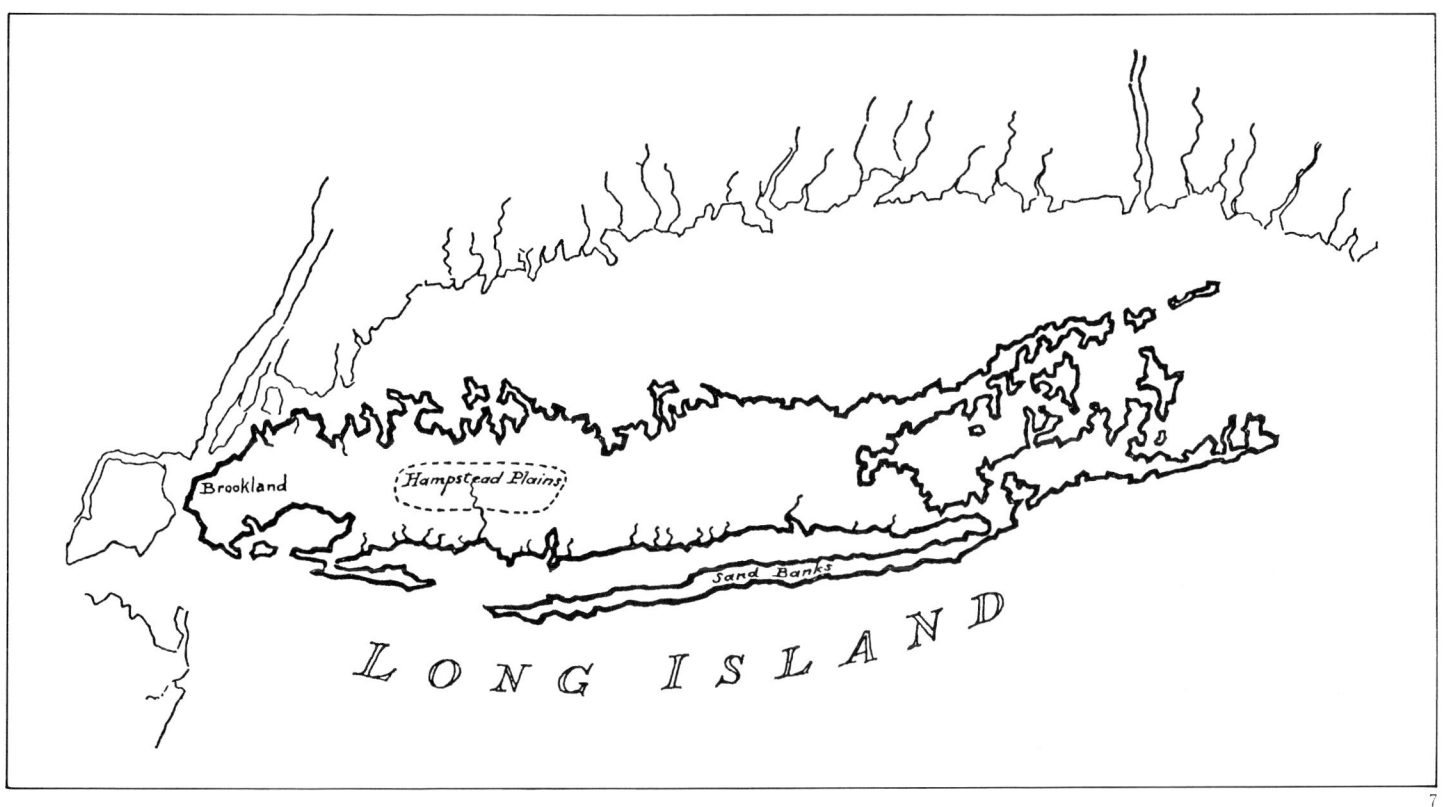

7. The Hempstead Plains. This section of the Morden map, published in London in 1720, suggests that the Hempstead Plains looked unusual to early mapmakers and settlers. It was said of this huge, treeless expanse of undulating grass in the middle of the heavily wooded island that "its appearance from its borders strongly resembled that of a lake" (Timothy Dwight, *Travels*). Daniel Denton wrote in 1670 in his *Brief Description of New York*: "Toward the middle of Long Island lyeth a plain sixteen miles long and four broad, upon which grows very fine grass that makes exceeding good Hay and is very good pasture for sheep and other Cattel." For the next hundred-odd years, the Plains were used for this purpose by the Town of Hempstead, but when the livestock industry moved to the Western prairies these thousands of landlocked acres lay unused. After years of vacillating between dividing the land and selling it, the State Legislature in 1867 authorized "the Freeholders and Electors of the Town of Hempstead, Queens County, State of New York, to sell their common land or any portion thereof" (Laws of the State of New York, Chapter 639).

8

8. The Birdfoot Violet. Little Ruth Velcor has climbed down from her grandmother's carriage to pick some of the birdfoot violets that carpeted the Hempstead Plains in early May each year. Winter over, the Plains in those days lay flat, dry and welcoming to horse and carriage. During the Ice Age, the Plains had gradually been formed by glacial outwash, slowly accumulating a fragile layer of soil and producing new varieties of plant life. The most spectacular, in both abundance and color, was the birdfoot violet (*Viola pedata*). Close to the ground, these clustered violets grew out of a circle of stemless leaves, each leaf segmented to form the pattern of a bird's foot. This lovely wildflower was still flourishing when A. T. Stewart purchased this vast tract. (*Nassau County Museum*)

9. The Stewart Purchase. The New York business community was amazed by the news on July 17, 1869, that Alexander Stewart had purchased the Hempstead Plains. The amount paid in cash (at $55 an acre) and the sheer size of the Plains made it the biggest land deal of the century. *Harper's Weekly* later featured the story and helpfully included this map showing the Hempstead Plains in relation to the established villages of Hempstead, Mineola, Westbury and Bethpage, which bordered it. To quote: "The purchase of Hempstead Plains—a tract of land in the interior of Long Island, consisting of 7,000 acres—by Mr. A. T. Stewart was ratified by the citizens of Hempstead July 17. . . . This tract cost Mr. Stewart $400,000; and we understand that it is his design to spend from six to ten millions of dollars in the erection upon it of homes for the working-classes of New York and Brooklyn. This design is so gigantic that it throws into the shade every attempt of the kind hitherto made. With the improvements which Mr. Stewart will carry out; with a township of beautiful and healthful homes; with parks, gardens, and public buildings for educational purposes and for those of amusement, Hempstead Plains, hitherto a desert, will be made to blossom as the rose; it will be the most beautiful suburb in the vicinity of New York. God speed the undertaking!"

10. John Kellum, 1809–1871. Alexander Stewart and his architect and friend John Kellum spent the winter of 1869–1870 drawing up the master plan of the village and laying out in detail the central section between Rockaway Road and Franklin Avenue, which was to be developed first. (Areas to the east and west were to be used temporarily as farmland.) Kellum was a native and former resident of Hempstead; he was acquainted with the Town "fathers" and knew the history of the Hempstead Plains, and it was he who had alerted Stewart to the availability of this great tract of land. At this time he was a partner in the firm of Kirby & Kellum in New York, credited with designing the New York Court House, the Herald Building and the Friends' Meeting House. As Stewart's architect, he had designed the Great Iron Store on Broadway (see no. 3) and Stewart's $1,500,000 "Marble Palace" on Fifth Avenue (no. 4). This practical and talented man was indispensable to the multimillionaire merchant and was equally responsible for much of the planning and success of Garden City. He died suddenly two years later, leaving plans and designs for most of Garden City's important buildings—the hotel, the station, the stable and carriage house and the largest houses (to be known as the "Apostles"). They all represent his choice of the classical Victorian style, influenced by the great French architect François Mansart.

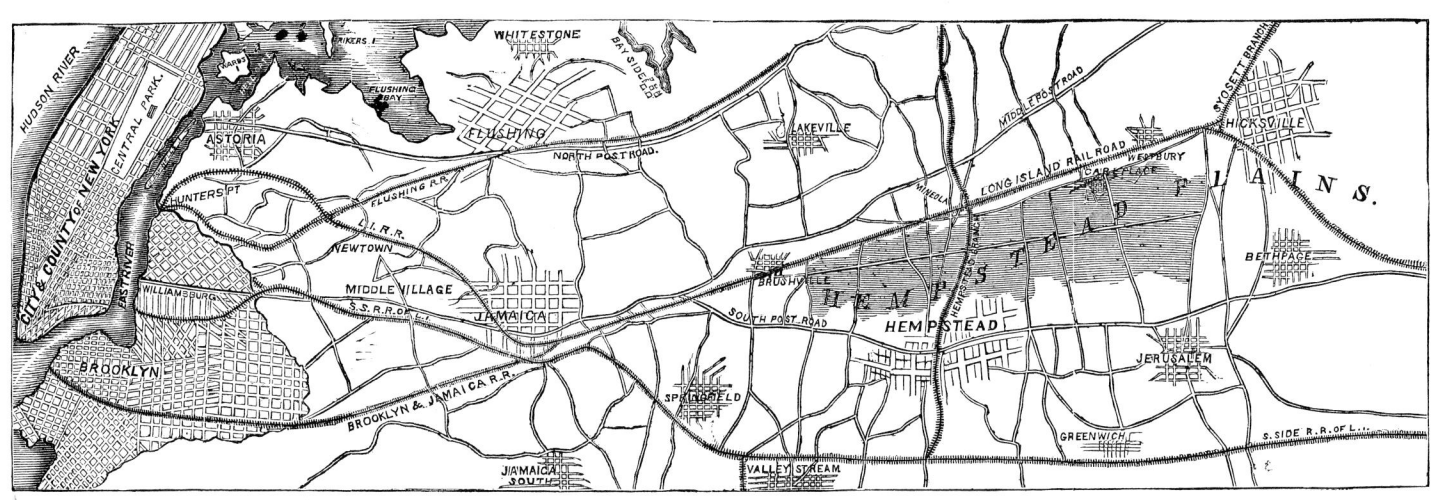

9

10

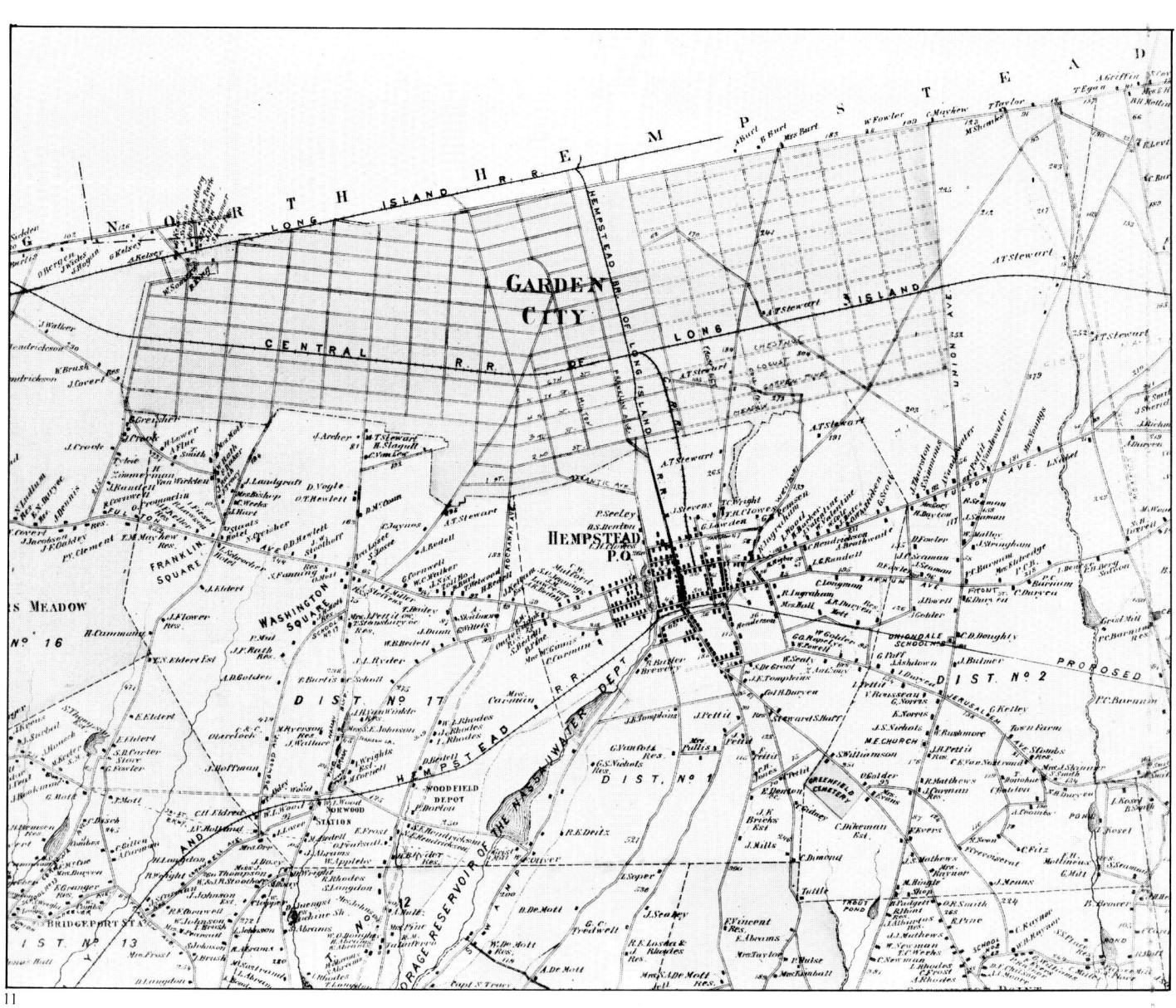

11. Garden City Master Plan. This 1873 map, with the rectangular grid-patterned area labeled "Garden City," shows how quickly Stewart had carried out his promise to the Town of Hempstead to develop the "barren waste" he had purchased. The new village was to be located between Mineola and Old Country Road on the north and the irregular border of Hempstead on the south. Though the eastern and western borders are only vaguely indicated, the master plan included approximately 5.2 square miles, the area of Garden City today. Of special interest is Stewart's Central Railroad of Long Island, which he had built to run through the heart of the village and which continued east through the Hempstead Plains to his brickworks at Bethpage. This ensured transportation for the "Stewart bricks" he was to use for all public buildings in the village. More important for the future was the Hempstead Branch line (center), which ran north–south and parallel to the old Mineola Branch line to Hempstead. It is still in use today. At the upper left, the Central Railroad tracks curve westward to Floral Park. In those days the line continued through Queens to Flushing; there, through an arrangement with the Flushing and North Side Railroad, trains could run to Hunters Point for connection by ferry to 34th Street or Wall Street.

THE PLANNED VILLAGE

12. The First House. In the spring of 1870 the first house was built in Garden City—a large two-story Victorian building with a sturdy, windowed cupola. Located on Rockaway Avenue and 1st Street, it faced the treeless, empty acres that were to be the site of the new village. This became the administrative headquarters of architect John Kellum and Delamater Denton, head of the engineering firm Stewart had chosen to carry out his plans. By July, surveyors were fanning out over the roughly graded land, charting the roadbed for the railroad and staking out the broad avenues and streets. Gradually the outlines of the village emerged, as fifteen miles of picket fencing began to surround each 1000′ × 500′ block. By the end of the year, John Kellum could point out just where the hotel, stable, waterworks, stores and big houses would be located. Years later, this building was remodeled as a residence; in 1960 it was replaced by a group of three houses.

13

14

15

13. James H. L'Hommedieu. To quote from Munsell's 1882 *History of Queens County*, "James H. L'Hommedieu erected every building in Garden City and the Cathedral as well." This was quite true, although the Cathedral, the bishop's residence and St. Paul's School were not yet completed. The rest of the structures—hotel, stable, stores, houses, station, waterworks—had all been built by this reliable and talented man, and after John Kellum's death he had even designed some of them. Born on a farm in Smithtown, he had little formal education, but was so capable as an apprentice to a carpenter/builder that everyone expected that "he would someday be an architect of ability and reputation." He worked briefly in New York, married and moved back to Great Neck, where he established a successful building operation. In 1869 Stewart chose him to take charge of all construction. His good relationship with Stewart extended to Stewart's lawyer Judge Hilton, Mrs. Stewart and the two architects of the Cathedral buildings. When his work in Garden City was completed, L'Hommedieu enlarged his building and contracting operations in Great Neck and became an important supplier of building equipment.

14. The Grand Hotel, 1874. Hotels were important to Alexander Stewart. He owned three in New York City and one, the Grand Union Hotel, in Saratoga. In planning his new village, he intended the hotel in its 23-acre landscaped park to be its central feature, with avenues and streets leading to it and his Central Railroad at its doorstep. Designed by John Kellum in the stately French Victorian style, it was completed in 1874 at a cost of $125,000. The ground floor was given over to drawing and dining rooms, ladies' parlors and gentlemen's card and billiard rooms. The upper floors housed the twenty-five guest rooms and the private suite for the Stewarts and their guests. Here was the reality at last—the grand hotel Stewart had promised from the first. On its opening day in July, distinguished guests, friends and reporters crowded into the handsome rooms, each with its own marble fireplace. They marveled at the rich carpets, hangings, mirrors and rosewood or black-walnut pieces from his great New York store. The hotel was pronounced a great success, and with it the new village. As young John Van DeWater of Hempstead wrote in his news sheet: "For a young place Garden City is going along bravely. It already has a large brick hotel, many first-class dwellings, stores, a gas works, street lamps and other modern improvements." More than a hundred years later, a Garden City Hotel is still welcoming guests in the same spot, in a smaller park.

15. The Stable and Carriage House, 1874. On the south side of 7th Street, conveniently near the new hotel, James L'Hommedieu built an impressive two-story, 130-foot-long brick carriage house and stable. An unusual feature was the entrance driveway, which ran straight through the central section of the building to a big stableyard behind. The mansard-roofed wings on either side provided ample space for the thirty-six stalls and the tack and harness rooms, and wide areas for carriages of all kinds. As an added convenience, a boardinghouse for coachmen and stable staff was built at the corner of Franklin Avenue. Horse-drawn phaetons, buggies and surreys (open or canopytop) carried hotel guests to the Meadow Brook Hunt Club, Belmont's Turf and Field Club, neighboring villages and the beaches. Over the years, saddle horses, hunters, polo ponies and matched pairs were stabled here as well. This handsome building was to serve the hotel and community for many years, and was completely renovated in 1927 as the first Village Hall.

The Planned Village 11

16

18

19

12

16. A "Whisky Gig," 1880. This handsome two-wheeler gig has just left the stableyard behind the 7th Street stable and carriage house and is passing the large barn behind Poole's emporium on Hilton Avenue. (This road still runs between the two store blocks to Hilton Avenue, but is now paved and is used as an access to the parking field.) The high-stepping horse suggests that this light carriage is a "Whisky gig"—one that, according to the catalogue of Suffolk Museum's Carriage House, "travels so fast it seems to whisk down the road." Its chairlike body hangs on leather braces that are attached to the long shafts. The driver wears a formal hat and carries a whip; his destination is unknown.

17. The Garden City Station, c. 1873. Like all the important buildings in the new village, the railroad station managed to have at least a token mansard roof. As part of the cupola, it rose above the impressive front entrance and was crowned with ornamental ironwork. This square one-story building, completed in 1873, housed not only the ticket office but the village's first post office (later moved to Poole's general store on Hilton Avenue). To protect passengers entering or leaving the train, a long, sheltering roof covering a broad platform was attached to the rear of the station. John Kellum designed this small building to complement the large, square hotel which it faced at the end of a treelined avenue. It was torn down in 1898 and a fountain, in a small circular park, was installed on the site to face the hotel instead. A new and larger station was built to the west, and is still in use today (see no. 60).

18. A Central Railroad Locomotive. This very early photograph shows a group of proud engineers and admirers posing with one of A. T. Stewart's locomotives at the Garden City depot. The identity of the engine is uncertain, but it is believed to be either the Hempstead No. 12, built in 1873 by Brooks, or the Garden City No. 10, built in 1872 by the Rhode Island Locomotive Works. Both were commissioned for the Central Railroad, along with a rolling stock of sixteen new cars. Service on the new line began on the morning of January 8, 1873, and provided nine trains daily between Hempstead and Long Island City, where ferries to New York were available. According to Vincent Seyfried, historian of the L.I.R.R., "the Central Rail Road also began furnishing Pullman Palace Car service on the road in 1874, as well as weekend excursions to Garden City to allow prospective tenants to look over the Village." Fares to Garden City were 45 cents, to Hempstead 50 cents.

19. The Newtown No. 6. In the early days of railroading, steam locomotives were looked upon with a great deal of pride, and were often elaborately decorated to observe national events and holidays. Following President Lincoln's assassination, for example, many were heavily draped in black. The Newtown No. 6, above, is more cheerfully decked out for the 4th of July. Built in 1871 by the Rhode Island Locomotive Works, it was used on the Central Railroad for a few years, but was later taken over by the L.I.R.R.

20. The Estate Building, c. 1875. "A. T. Stewart's Garden City, L. I. New winter and summer residences with gardens attached, and containing all the modern conveniences and improvements. Rents from $250 to $1,000 per annum, according to size and quality of the house and grounds." It was hoped that advertisements such as this in New York papers would bring prospective tenants to the new village on Stewart's railroad. The station had been completed in 1873, but an estate office was sorely needed. In 1875 James L'Hommedieu built this elaborate mansard-roofed building just to the north of the station, where W. R. Hinsdale, the agent, could welcome newcomers. In the rooms above were kept village records, documents, maps and blueprints, which had been transferred from the earlier headquarters on Rockaway Avenue. These were all lost in 1911 when fire completely destroyed the building.

21. An "Apostle" House, 1877. This early photograph was taken on June 28, 1877, the day the cornerstone of the Cathedral was laid (see no. 34). Partially framed arches for the Cathedral's south wall can be seen at the right of this handsome "Apostle" house, which was to be moved to make way for the bishop's residence. Nine identical homes, the first and largest dwellings to be built in the new village, were completed in 1872 at a cost of $18,000 apiece, each three stories high with mansard roof and distinguishing cupola. Designed by John Kellum to complement the stately hotel, and located on large 250′ × 250′ lots, they epitomized, as they do today, the elegance and taste demanded by A. T. Stewart. Generous planting, a surrounding picket fence and a three-stall carriage house with coachman's quarters above were also part of their luxurious settings. Six still remain—three on Rockaway Road, one on Cathedral Avenue, one on Hilton Avenue and one (now headquarters of the Historical Society) on 5th Street. As legend has it, these houses were named "Apostles" (and the later, smaller ones "Disciples") by students of the two Cathedral schools, who temporarily lived in them until their own buildings were completed.

22. A Brick "Disciple" House, c. 1875. Because Stewart's large brickworks in Bethpage were connected by spur to his Central Railroad, brick had been used extensively in his planned village, not only for the hotel but for the railroad station, stable and carriage house, stores and waterworks. But the houses, although built on brick foundations, were all sheathed in narrow clapboard siding. The exceptions were to be the last five houses that Stewart commissioned. Designed earlier by John Kellum, they were built of brick, scaled-down versions of the three-story, mansard-roofed "Apostle" houses, but without cupolas; instead, charming small porches were added. All had neat carriage houses to the rear of their deep lots. They were a welcome addition to the attractive frame houses along the treelined streets. Four still remain—two on 6th Street, one on 9th and the house above on Hilton Avenue. These five and several other big houses that were used by Cathedral-school students as temporary housing have been called "Disciples" even to this day.

21

22

23–26. The Smaller Houses. In the four years from 1871 to 1875, A. T. Stewart built over eighty homes. In line with his feudal policy of keeping control of the entire village, these houses could only be rented, at an annual rate that depended on size and location. But all were constructed to high standards by James L'Hommedieu, built on generous lots surrounded by picket fences, provided with carriage houses or barns and located relatively near the stores and railroad station. All but the five brick "Disciples" were constructed of wood, with clapboard siding, and, according to the *Sentinel*, were "highly decorated chaste specimens of rural architecture." John Kellum had designed the "Apostle" houses to complement the hotel, but had adapted popular plans, in the Victorian style, for smaller homes and "villas" to create variety and individuality. A few of these two- or three-story houses were painted in various colors as well. Size, color and material might vary, but all had generous porches, many windows, handsome staircases, high-ceilinged rooms and a welcoming air. These features and their resulting charm have been the source of their appeal up to the present day. The forty-four surviving houses are included among the A. T. Stewart Era Buildings that were listed on the National Register of Historic Places in 1978.

23

24

25

26

27

28

18   *The Planned Village*

27. The First Stores. As part of Garden City's carefully planned commercial area, the first block of stores was built in 1873 on the east side of Hilton Avenue between 7th Street and the railroad tracks. The two-story brick building, designed by L'Hommedieu, housed five stores in a prim row, all under one long roof with a pediment in its center and with decorative double brackets supporting it. In front of the stores, bordering the wide avenue, hitching posts stood ready for the carriage trade. Over the years, these small stores housed a variety of merchants—Thomas Scott (pharmacist), the Ackley brothers (butchers), Willis Messereau (general merchant) and Mr. Grotzki (barber). Much later, Hubbell's real-estate office filled several of them, and in 1923 the Garden City Bank, occupying two small rooms next door, opened its doors to the public. The building, much altered by the addition of a third floor and a pillared entrance, still stands, and is now used for offices.

28. The Second Store Block. In 1875 a second block of stores was built on Hilton Avenue north of the railroad tracks—a square, two-story brick building in the Victorian style. Although rather severe, its symmetrical façade gave James L'Hommedieu the chance to indulge his taste for brickwork as a decorative feature around doors, windows and the arched roof line. It was divided into two large stores; one was soon rented as a drugstore, the other by E. C. Poole as an emporium for dry goods, groceries and general merchandise. In 1877, when the railroad station became too small for double duty, this store also became the village's second post office. The rooms above the stores were originally to be rented, but instead the large, sunny area above Poole's became Garden City's first public school, a one-room schoolhouse. Classes were held there until the "Little School" was built in 1902 at the end of 7th Street on Cathedral Avenue (see no. 76). The building, imaginatively restored and painted to emphasize its architectural features, is now used entirely for offices.

29. A Grammar School Class, c. 1889. A note from Kitty Briel's daughter accompanying this photograph reads: "My mother got into nearby Garden City Grammar School on April 1, 1890. She is not the teacher posing with the boys and girls. Here she taught the Dubroskies and other Polish children. When school closed in June, she noted that she weighed 113 pounds (5'5"); and that the average attendance at school was 32." In the one-room school, teachers earning salaries of eight dollars a week were faced with teaching children of widely differing ages. Miss Briel probably also had language problems with these pupils, who lived in the row of workmen's cottages on Franklin Avenue. But whatever their English abilities, all understood that recess was over when she rang the red-handled school bell at the open window above Poole's store each day.

The Planned Village 19

30. Workmen's Cottages, 1872. Built south of the railroad crossing on the east side of Franklin Avenue as far down as 5th Street, these eighteen cottages housed the families of the skilled workmen imported from the city to build Stewart's planned village. Since eastern Queens County was still largely agricultural in 1869, local labor could not provide enough experienced carpenters, masons, bricklayers, roofers, joiners or plasterers for this large-scale project. The families, many of them Polish and new to America, were only too glad to be provided with financial security and undreamed-of housing—each cottage having seven rooms, cellar and furnace, gaslight and running water. It was for the children of these families that Garden City's first public school was started. Years later, when Doubleday, Page and Company bought the forty acres along Franklin Avenue for its Country Life Press, these well-built, attractive houses were moved to a newly developed area between Meadow Street and Franklin Court. Completely remodeled and enlarged, they are now a part of the residential area called Franklin Court West.

31. The Waterworks, 1876. From the first, Alexander Stewart had planned a municipal water system for Garden City. By September 1876 it was completed, putting an end to villagewide dependence on wells and hand pumps. In this photograph, the great well, fifty feet in diameter and forty feet deep, is at the right, shielded by a charming brick wellhouse. It had been laboriously dug on a site at the end of Cherry Valley Avenue and 11th Street, a quarter of a mile from the heart of the village. In the center is the large brick and limestone-trimmed structure, resembling

a medieval castle, that was designed and built by James L'Hommedieu. It housed the machinery of the Holly system, which pumped water into the seven miles of pipe throughout the village. The engineer's house, on the left, completed the new waterworks. On November 9, 1876, the formal opening took place, and the day was celebrated with pageantry and pomp. As a brass band played, Hempstead firemen attached hoses to the new hydrants for the test. The pressure sent the water high into the air—up to 165 feet—to the delight of the spectators, among them Mrs. Stewart and Judge Hilton. The great well and the engineer's house were demolished in the 1950s. But the handsome main building, in a landscaped setting of trees and shrubs, is still in use today as a control center for Garden City's battery of wells.

32. Panorama of Garden City, 1878. It is safe to date this unusual wide-angle photograph because the Cathedral is still without its spire. Safe, too, to say that it was taken from the windowed cupola or roof of John Kellum's headquarters on Rockaway Avenue. This old, established road, which ran north to the Queens County courthouse, is at the left; it formed, at that time, the western boundary of the new village, which stretched eastward to Franklin Avenue. The two tall "Apostle" houses in the foreground are still in place today, as are most of the houses visible on Hilton Avenue and streets nearby. The hotel can just be glimpsed behind and to the right of the Cathedral. In the distance, the Manhasset Hills form the uneven horizon. In ten years' time, the promised "City on the Plain" had become a reality.

THE MEMORIAL CATHEDRAL

33

33. Cornelia Clinch Stewart, 1803–1886. Cornelia Clinch Stewart, wife of A. T. Stewart, was a remarkable woman in her own right. Being childless, she was able to share more fully in her husband's interests and projects: his grand hotel in Saratoga, his Great Iron Store, his trips to Europe for business and collecting art, and his purchase of the Hempstead Plains and founding of Garden City. As a result, when he died in 1876 she was experienced and involved enough not only to continue the development of the village but to make a contribution of lasting importance herself. This was to plan, build and endow, as a memorial to her husband, a foundation for the Episcopal Diocese of Long Island consisting of the Cathedral of the Incarnation, two Cathedral schools and a bishop's residence. She was seventy-one years old when she initiated these bold plans, and, with the help of her friend and lawyer Judge Henry Hilton, spent the last ten years of her life carrying them out. The project was to revitalize the newly built village and turn Garden City into America's first cathedral town. She died in 1886 and is buried in the crypt of the Cathedral. This portrait was painted in 1844 by Edward Dalton Marchant (1806–1877). (*Heckscher Museum, Huntington, L.I.*)

34. Cathedral Cornerstone Laying. This early glass plate photograph, discovered in the Deanery attic, was taken looking northwest on June 28, 1877, when the cornerstone of the Cathedral of the Incarnation was laid. To the left are the walls and arched windows of the great building already under construction; in the center, the tents for the ceremony; and behind them, a long line of waiting railroad passenger cars. (Three trainloads had been required to bring the crowds from Brooklyn and New York.) Cathedral Avenue and the southwest corner of 5th Street are in the foreground. Newspapers later estimated the attendance in the thousands. Several hundred took part in the ceremonial march, banners flying, from the hotel to the site. The procession was led by a uniformed band and consisted of Sunday-school children, choristers, vestrymen, deaconesses, clergy, deputies, prominent laity, corporators of the Cathedral and visiting bishops. The solemn celebration of the building of the Cathedral, a memorial church that was to serve as the seat of the Episcopal Diocese of Long Island, was conducted by Bishop Abram N. Littlejohn.

35. The Cathedral of the Incarnation. This 1886 photograph shows the cruciform decorated-Gothic Cathedral proudly standing on its forty-acre park in a small village (population 550) built on the flat, treeless Hempstead Plains. To the northwest is the imposing Cathedral School of St. Paul, large enough to accommodate 300 students. Garden City had been called Stewart's Folly; now some felt that this million-dollar church might be Bishop Littlejohn's. Architecturally interesting is the use, by the architect Henry G. Harrison, of cast-iron beams and molded-iron columns as supporting elements. As a result, the exterior buttressing could be greatly reduced and slender columns in the nave and clerestory could be used to support the high, vaulted ceiling. The Cathedral is built of Belleville, N. J., brownstone, and is 175 feet long and 96 feet wide. It has steep, slate-covered roofs, an 80-foot bell tower and above it a tapering 130-foot spire crowned with an illuminated brass cross. James L'Hommedieu, who had built all the other buildings in Garden City, was in charge of its construction, which took eight years to complete. It stands in the heart of the village between Cathedral Avenue and Rockaway Road.

36. Cathedral Interior. This view of the nave of the Cathedral is from the chancel looking toward the open entrance doors. Slender pillars with decorated bases and molded capitals support the arches and intricate stone vaulting of the 53-foot-high ceiling. Light is streaming in through the stained-glass windows, which had been commissioned in 1882 from the London firm of Claydon, Bell and Company. Out of sight is the great $50,000 Hilborne L. Roosevelt organ, as is the specially designed furniture. The entire structure has been carefully guarded and maintained for over one hundred years; as a result, the interior looks much the same today, although fixed pews now rest on the marble floor and a new organ was installed in 1985.

37. The Crypt. The polygonal marble crypt, located under the chancel of the Cathedral, is seen in all its beauty in this drawing by a newspaper staff artist. Marble pillars support the vaulted ribs to form a domelike ceiling twenty feet in height. The stained-glass windows were made by the London firm of Heaton, Butler and Boyne. The drawing also suggests the concern, wonder and curiosity felt by the public at this time. For the Memorial Cathedral that was to be Alexander Stewart's final resting place was still under construction in 1878 when graverobbers stole his body from the family vault in the graveyard of St.-Mark's-in-the-Bowery. During the following months confusion reigned—clues were found, rumors abounded, ransoms were supposedly paid and newspapers provided the public with every detail of this bizarre case. In 1881, according to legend, a young relative of Mrs. Stewart was able to recover the body and have it brought to the Cathedral; the truth of this story has never been confirmed. When Mrs. Stewart died, she too was buried in the crypt, and the large marble commemorative urn seen in the drawing was placed in the center of the light-filled room.

38. The Bishop's Residence. The *New York Sun* of June 26, 1884, relates: "Bishop Littlejohn of the Protestant Episcopal Diocese of Long Island moved from his home in Remsen Street, Brooklyn, yesterday, to his 32-room residence provided for him in Garden City. The building is of brick with free-stone trim and is four stories in height. It looks toward the Cathedral and is in a park laid out around it. The visitor descends from his carriage in a porte cochere, climbs a short flight of stairs to a large square hall. The eye is attracted first by a large stained glass window looking toward the Cathedral. In the centre is a bishop's mitre, with crossed key and crosier behind it. The design is softened by half tints and shadings of color." The article goes on to describe the opulence of the furnishing of the principal rooms—woodwork of San Domingo mahogany, floors of oak with mosaic borders of black walnut, high ceilings with plasterwork and brass hanging lamps. Also "choice mantels and furniture obtained from dealers in curious and antique furniture," and chairs and sofas upholstered in figured silk, velvet, silk plush or tapestry. As the photograph shows, it was a large house, and seven rooms on the fourth floor would be needed for servants. Far to the rear of the residence, on 4th Street, a brick stable with quarters for the coachman had been built. According to the article, "there were six stalls and in one of them yesterday the Bishop's horse munched oats as though he had come to stay." The building is now used as the Diocesan center. (*Nassau County Museum*)

39. Laying the Cornerstone of St. Paul's School, 1879. This drawing by a *Leslie's* staff artist of the "Ceremony of Laying the Corner-stone of the 'Cathedral School of St. Paul'," June 18, 1879, shows Bishop Littlejohn officiating before a large gathering of visiting clergy, corporators of the Cathedral and choristers (left). Seated at the right are Mrs. Stewart, her brother Charles Clinch and Judge Hilton, with members of her family behind. Although it was June, a large protective tent covered the area, and a wooden flooring had been laid. It was to take James L'Hommedieu four years to construct this imposing, 260-foot-long, brick Victorian Gothic building—four stories in height and crowned with a slate mansard roof and a clock and bell tower. The E-shaped structure was to contain a chapel seating 400, an assembly hall, a library, laboratories, a dining hall, dormitory quarters for 300 students and suites for the headmaster and staff. Set well back on a landscaped forty-acre site on Stewart Avenue and bounded by Rockaway Road on the east, it proved a fitting complement to the tall-spired Cathedral. The architect was E. H. Harris, who also designed the bishop's residence.

40

41

42

40. Military Exercises, St. Paul's School, 1884. Here, in front of St. Paul's School, we see cadets at attention watching luckier fellow-cadets firing off the cannon that the Government had provided for instruction in artillery drill. A U.S. Army officer stands by, giving orders and keeping control of the exercise. Even before the school building was completed in 1883, a military department of cadets had been organized into two companies, with a full complement of officers. Now infantry training had been expanded to include proficiency in cannon drill. As headquarters, an "Armory" had been set up in a large basement area of the building. For uniforms, the cadets wore unusually handsome two-toned blue outfits with brass buttons bearing the arms of the Diocese. Military training was dropped ten years later. St. Paul's went on to develop into one of the leading preparatory schools in the east; now, over a hundred years later, it is still flourishing, and its imposing, well-maintained building and campus are one of Garden City's chief attractions.

41. St. Paul's Football Team. Along with military training and a rigorous classical education, students were also busy with such sports as football, baseball and ice hockey. A letter from a student to a family friend, dated October 30, 1884, gives us a glimpse of those early days:

> Dear Mr. Hayes;
> I am very sorry to . . . decline your very kind invitation to dine with you next Saturday, as I do not think Mr. Frisby would like me to stay in town so late on that day. Garden City begins to assume its wintry and dismal aspect, there is nothing cheering to be seen except the picture of George W. Childs in the billiard room of the hotel, which picture I remember you admired greatly when you came to see me last year.
> Though our pond is not very large yet it is large enough to play shin[n]y on, and I hope that we may have the pleasure of barking each other['s] shins in that noble game this winter. Hoping to see you soon . . . I remain
>
> Your affectionate small friend
> James W. Gerard Jr.

Here the football team of 1885, champions of the New York area, poses for a formal portrait.

42. The Cathedral School of St. Mary. Although E. H. Harris drew up plans for both schools at the same time, St. Mary's School was not built until 1892. Until then, its students lived and carried out all academic activities in several large houses near the Cathedral. The cornerstone was laid in May, and by the end of the year James L'Hommedieu had all but completed this large brick-and-brownstone building on a beautiful site east of Cathedral Avenue between 4th and 5th Streets. (An "Apostle" house originally located there was moved to the north side of 5th Street, where it is now used by the Historical Society.) Although St. Mary's was smaller than St. Paul's, the rooms of St. Mary's were attractively arranged and furnished, special features being suites for students, a large studio and cooking-class facilities. The curriculum was similar in the two schools, with an emphasis on Latin, mathematics, geography, science and "sacred studies." Four years of French were required, but Greek was optional. With its handsome new building, St. Mary's soon became as popular and successful a preparatory school as St. Paul's. Although no longer a boarding school, it is still sending its graduates to colleges and universities.

43. Consecration of the Cathedral. Since photographers were unwelcome during religious services, *Harper's Weekly* sent a staff artist to Garden City on June 2, 1885, to record the consecration of the Memorial Cathedral of the Incarnation. This drawing depicts the climax of the long, impressive ceremony, and suggests the solemnity of the occasion. At left is the frail, elderly widow, dressed in deep mourning, presenting to Bishop Littlejohn the deed of donation which transfers the title of the land, the Cathedral, the see house and the schools to the Episcopal diocese. At her left is Judge Henry Hilton, her friend and legal adviser. The bishop stands before the great altar, where the document will be placed in the presence of the clergy and the large gathering. Carved woodwork and stained-glass windows can be seen in the background. On June 2, 1985, a similar service of reconsecration was held in the Cathedral, one of the many events of a yearlong celebration of its centennial.

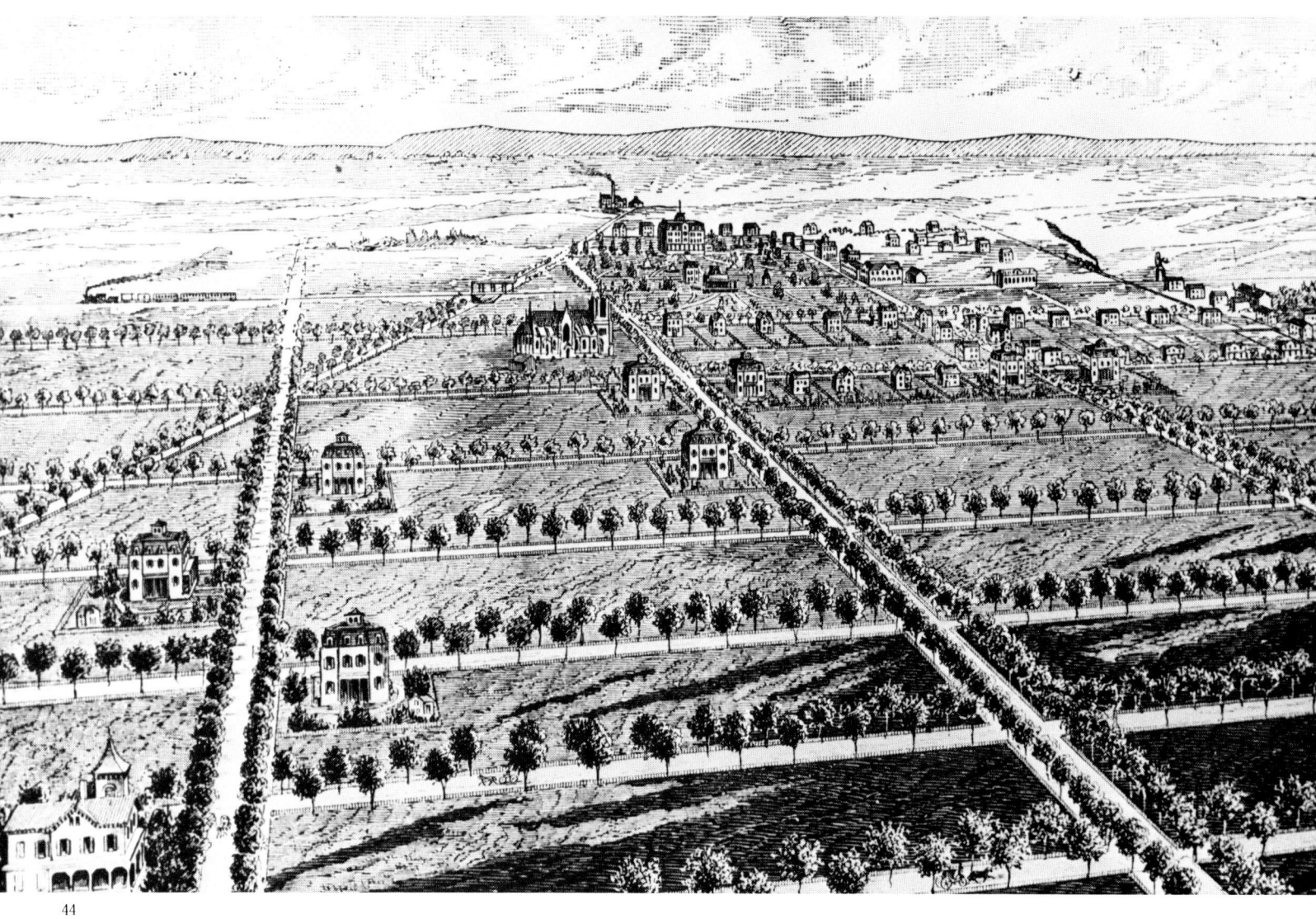

44

44. View of the Village, c. 1878. This drawing gives us a detailed look at Stewart's planned village, including the still-spireless cathedral that Mrs. Stewart built in his memory. The artist shows us in detail each road and avenue lined with picket fencing and methodically planted trees. The hotel (upper center) looks suitably important. We see Stewart's steam train (upper left), with its coal car and freight and passenger cars, on its busy way to New York. At far right, a smaller train heads for Hempstead on the old Mineola Branch line. At top center, the waterworks is busy providing water to the village from the great well. Several "Apostle" houses are visible toward the foreground, along with sixty or more middle-sized and smaller houses. Many of the buildings in this drawing have been preserved and cherished and are still in use. In 1978 these A. T. Stewart Era Buildings, built 1871–1893, received recognition as a "thematic group" in the National Register of Historic Places.

THE GARDEN CITY COMPANY

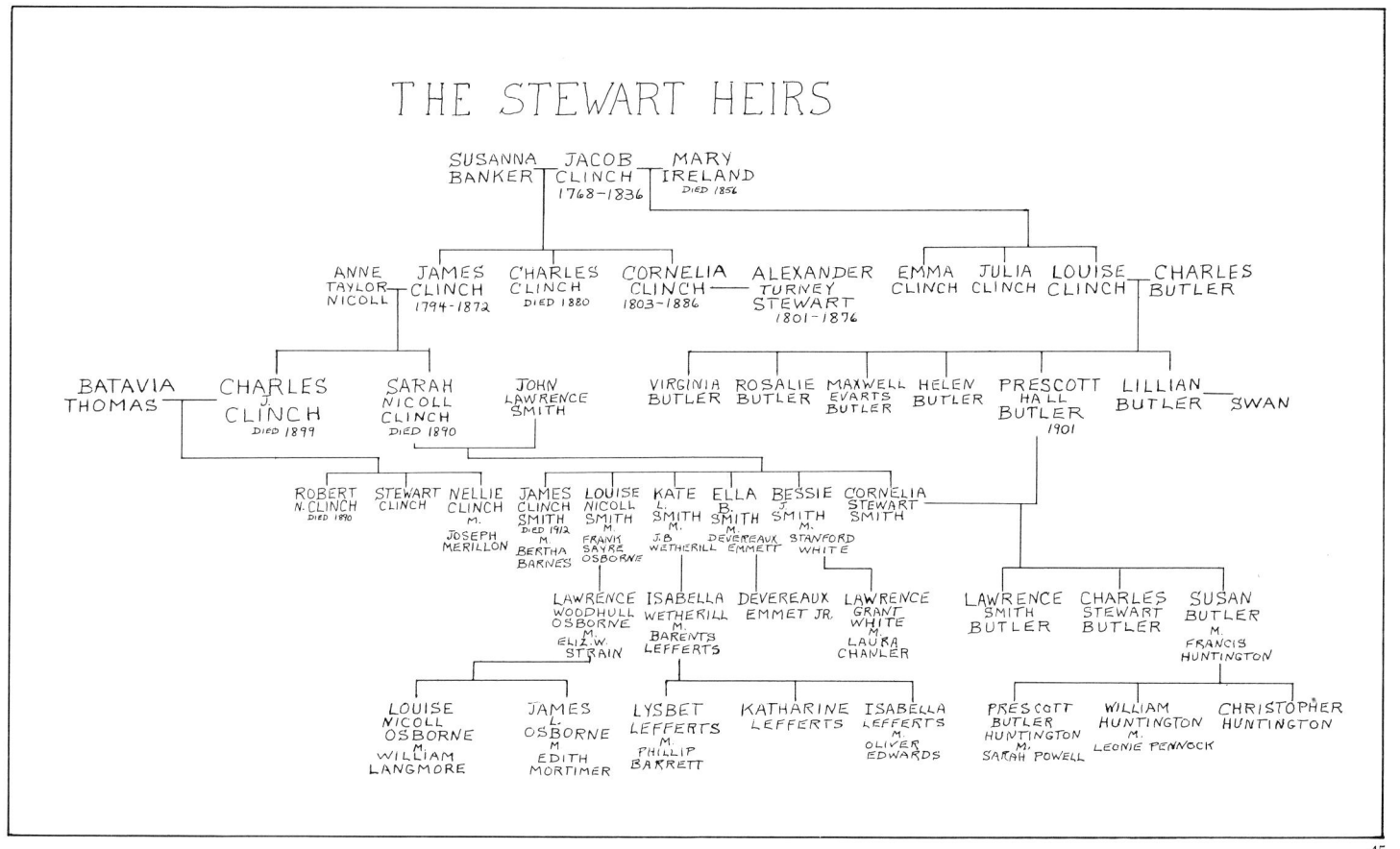

45. The Stewart Heirs. Mrs. Stewart died in 1886 at the age of 83. Being childless, she left a large part of her estate to her brother's children and grandchildren; the rest remained under the control of Henry Hilton, her lawyer, who was to carry out her projects concerning the Cathedral. After several years of litigation a settlement was achieved in 1893, and her heirs inherited not only many of the New York properties but over 7500 acres of the Hempstead Plains, including the village itself. Deciding to take "title in common" for partition of the property, the heirs incorporated the 5000 acres east of Clinton Road separately as the Merillon and Hempstead Plains Companies and the 2600 acres to the west as the Garden City Company. This they would develop under the more worldly and liberal policy of selling land outside the family. The officers and directors of the Garden City Company were Charles Clinch, Allen Evarts, Maxwell Butler, Horace Russell, James Clinch Smith, Devereux Emmet, Frank Sayre Osborne and Stanford White (see no. 49). To quote from a press release: "It will be the aim of the company to make Garden City as complete and attractive a country resort as there is anywhere. We have a fine settlement to begin with: good water works, a gas plant and many handsome residences. The new company will build houses for sale or rent. It will sell land to persons who are desirable as residents in such a community and will lend them money to build houses. In every way possible we shall endeavor to extend and improve Garden City so that persons doing business in New York or Brooklyn will find it desirable and agreeable to go there to live. Of course the company will retain control of the business section in order to prevent the intrusion of objectionable elements."

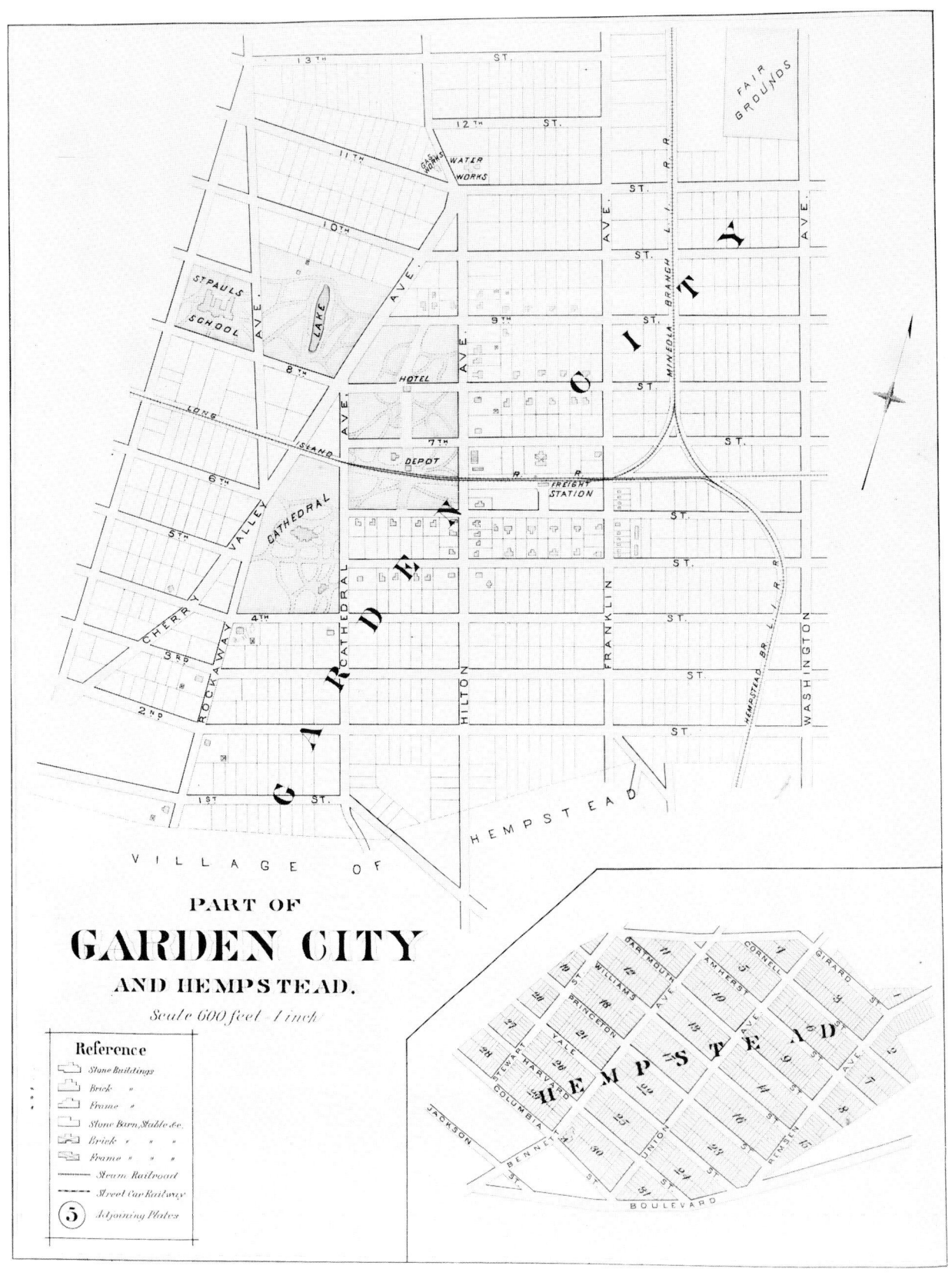

46. Garden City, 1888. This Chester Woolverton map, dated 1888 (published in his 1891 *Atlas*), represents the small central section of Garden City which Mr. and Mrs. Stewart had developed and which her heirs inherited in 1893. It seems to have all the necessities for a successful community: excellent rail transportation (center), water- and gasworks (top center), a hotel and stores (center) and sixty or more houses on treelined streets. It also had a famous cathedral and two growing church schools. But rumors persisted that Garden City was a "failure" and was hopelessly "long on land and short on residents." In fact, there was little incentive for families to settle in a community where renting was the only option, where an impersonal agent of a large estate was in control and where the only recreation was an annual fair at the County Fairgrounds (top right corner). To stimulate growth, the heirs decided to adopt a new policy of selling land, to remodel the hotel and casino, to develop recreational clubs and to expose Garden City to more worldly pleasures. The corporation, originally capitalized at $2,500,000, now invested a great deal more and immediately set to work to revitalize the village.

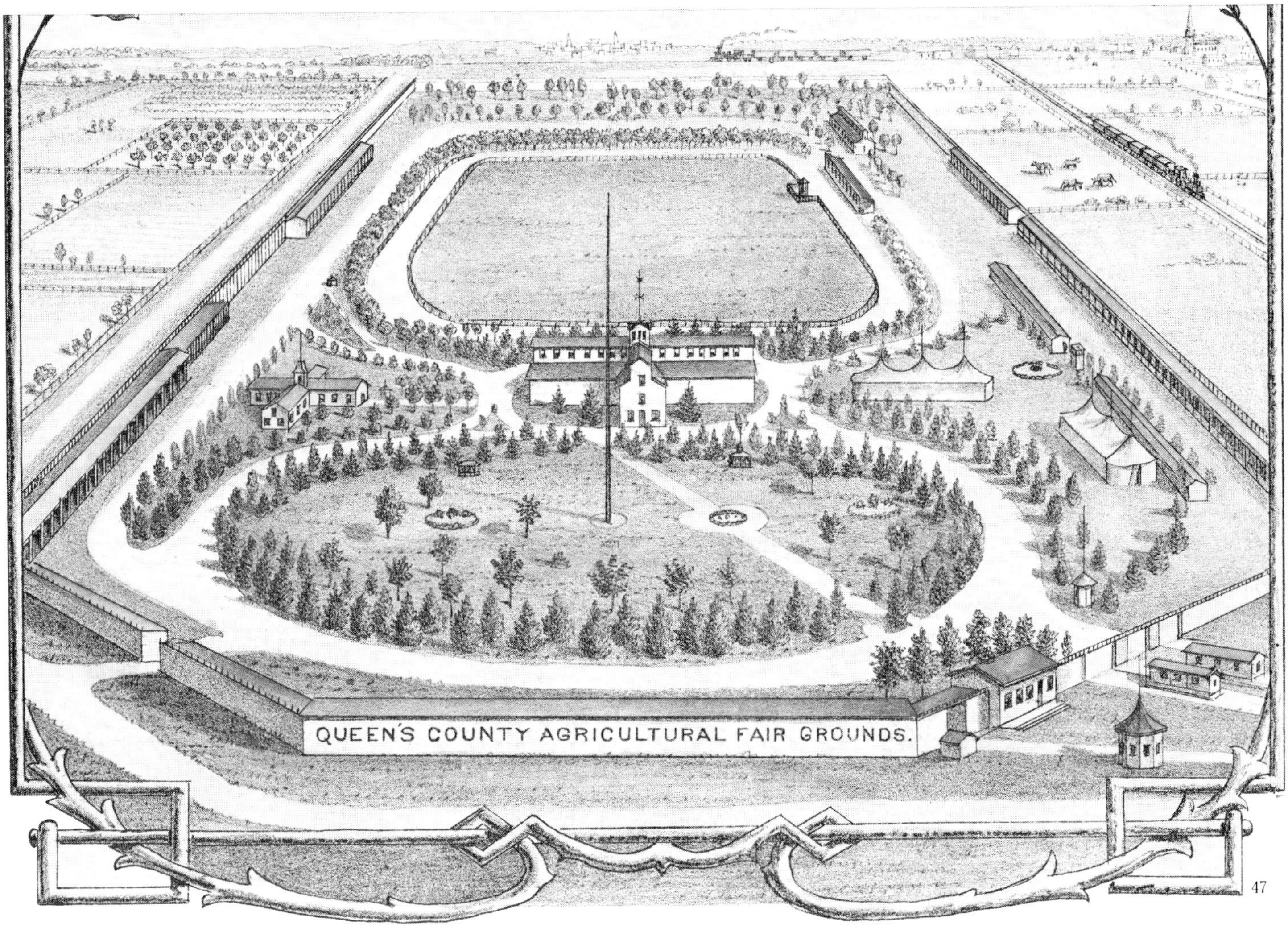

QUEEN'S COUNTY AGRICULTURAL FAIR GROUNDS.

47. The Fairgrounds, c. 1890. This detailed drawing (from W. W. Munsell's *History of Queens County*) portrays the fairgrounds of the Queens County Agricultural Society, which were built south of Old Country Road in 1866 and became a colorful part of Garden City life a few years later when Mr. Stewart built his village around it. This view faces south, with, at bottom right, the main entrance from Old Country Road; on either side, the roofed carriage sheds, reserved for members, marking the fairground boundaries; center, the great exhibition hall; to its left and right, poultry and livestock tents, buildings and sheds; and above, the racetrack, complete with judges' stand, stable and grandstand. Outside the fairgrounds, at left, is Washington Avenue; at right, the tracks of the Mineola–Hempstead railroad branch line, with steam train; and at top, Stewart's Central Railroad, with train. On the horizon is Hempstead, with its church spires, and at top right can be seen the Cathedral and Garden City. The grounds reverted to Nassau County in the 1950s, and are now the site of the County courthouse buildings.

48. The Meadow Brook Hunt Club. The Garden City Company's new policy of selling Stewart land made headlines in 1893 when it sold the large tract of land east of the village to the exclusive Meadow Brook Hunt Club, which had leased it for fourteen years. During that time, pink coats had been a common sight in the village, hunt breakfasts and dinner parties were held at the hotel, and young enthusiasts such as Elliott Roosevelt had rented houses for the season. Now the Club was to enlarge its clubhouse and stables, lay out a golf course and a second polo field and prepare for the great era of national and international polo matches on Long Island. (The illustration appeared in the October 20, 1877, issue of *The Daily Graphic*.)

The Garden City Company

49. Stanford White, 1853–1906. Married to Mrs. Stewart's grandniece Bessie Smith, daughter of Judge Lawrence Smith of Smithtown, Stanford White knew Garden City well. He had known the elderly Mrs. Stewart, had attended the consecration of the Cathedral and had stayed at Stewart's Victorian hotel. Inevitably, when the Garden City Company was formed, he became one of its directors (later vice president) and, as a partner in the famous architectural firm of McKim, Mead & White, was responsible for the stamp of taste and elegance that was to characterize the subsequent development of Garden City. Almost at once, he began the remodeling of the old hotel in the Georgian Revival style. It was just one of the many distinguished buildings this much-sought-after and prolific architect was to design for his firm over the years; in New York City alone, his name is associated with the Century and Metropolitan Clubs, the original Madison Square Garden, the American Yacht Club and the Washington Arch.

50. The Remodeled Hotel, c. 1895. Because of Stanford White's connection with the Garden City Company, the firm of McKim, Mead & White was chosen to remodel the old hotel when Cornelia Stewart's heirs assumed ownership of the village (see no. 14). Within a year, an elegant Georgian Revival redbrick building crowned with a "prettily designed cupola," with two new well-proportioned wings, had taken its place in the landscaped twenty-acre park. Large enough to house 200 guests, it provided welcoming piazzas, dining rooms overlooking the gardens, handsomely furnished reception and drawing rooms and elevator service to the rooms and suites above—ten with private bathrooms. For gentlemen, the basement provided billiard, smoking and card rooms and a well-stocked bar. Celebrations of the grand opening started with an elaborate ball and supper party, soon followed by the Meadow Brook Hunt Club's cotillion, in which, according to the *Hempstead Sentinel*, "only the smart set participated." Coaching parties, polo, gun and golf events, bicycle "runs" and tea dances were to keep the growing number of guests occupied. It was no surprise that the hotel register listed such prominent socialites as the Cushings, the Boardman Harrimans, the Belmonts, the Astors, the Pierpont Morgans, Charles F. Havemeyer and Mrs. Peter Cooper Hewitt. The remodeling, costing $150,000, had been a great success. And this small, beautiful hotel was to set the standards of taste and conservative elegance for the many large homes that were soon to be built in the village.

51, 52. The Hotel Interior, 1897. These photographs are from a small illustrated brochure advertising "the long established and newly enlarged Garden City Hotel, an elegant brick structure in the Georgian Revival style, beautifully furnished and exquisitely decorated." In no. 51 we see the parlor with its hanging ceiling lamp, oil paintings importantly framed against the flock-papered walls and the spinet piano ready for a lady's sure touch. No. 52 shows a bedroom, single here but available "en suite," with its enameled-iron-and-brass bedstead, flowered carpet and garlanded wallpaper.

54

36 *The Garden City Company*

53. The Casino, c. 1905. Located in the heart of Garden City at the corner of Cathedral Avenue and 6th Street, between the railroad station plaza (hidden, right) and the Cathedral (left), the Casino has played an important role in the village since 1885. Originally the Stewart Arms, an inn catering to out-of-town worshipers at the Cathedral, it became a modest tennis club with two grass courts. In 1895, financed by the Garden City Company, it was transformed by Stanford White into a fashionable, gray-shingled clubhouse with wide entrance porches, bay-windowed rooms and an open deck overlooking the new tennis courts. For indoor recreation it provided a large assembly hall, dining room and grill, card and billiard rooms, and two bowling alleys in the basement. With its remodeled clubhouse, the Garden City Casino, as it was now called, began its new role as a social and recreational club open to all residents. The formal opening took place on April 17, with a fashionable ball attended by the entire community and the directors of the Company. Ever since, it has been an indispensable club for all seasons and for every sort of village event. This view, looking west across the courts, is much the same today, though some changes have been made over the years—porches lost to interior expansion, chimneys rebuilt, the main entrance moved to 6th Street and the shingled exterior painted white.

54. Home of George Loring Hubbell. When the Garden City Company took over the village in 1893, George Loring Hubbell was already living there with his wife, involved in constructing the L.I.R.R.'s new branch line from Garden City to Valley Stream. Active in Cathedral and village affairs, he welcomed the Company's new policies and was the first to buy land and build his own house. (This house still stands at the corner of 1st Street and Cathedral Avenue.) Now involved in the Company as well, he was asked to join its ranks in 1896 as resident agent and manager. Able, enthusiastic, inventive and dedicated, he was subsequently to be invaluable to the development of the new hotel, the gun and golf clubs, the Casino, the new railroad station and even the first public-school building. He served the Company until Garden City was incorporated, at which time he became its mayor, and later a trustee.

The Garden City Company 37

55

56

55. The Garden City Golf Club. Golf at Meadow Brook and nearby Shinnecock proved so popular that in 1897 George Hubbell persuaded the Company to invest $1,500 in building a nine-hole subscription course of 3,000 yards on the rough, rolling, open land northwest of the new hotel. Immediately successful as the Island Golf Links ($15 season fee), it was enlarged to eighteen holes and incorporated May 17, 1899, as the Garden City Golf Club. It soon joined the U.S.G.A. and became the site of national and international competitions. Richard Howland Hunt, the well-known architect, designed its handsome clubhouse—a low, rambling buff-brick building with overhanging roof, open porches and the comforts of lounges, bar and dining and card rooms within. As to the course, it proved so varied and challenging—the "nearest to St. Andrews"—that even today it is listed as one of the hundred best courses in the world. Unlike others, it is still an "Eveless Eden," the ladies having left almost at once to join the Midland and Cherry Valley Clubs nearby. The clubhouse, somewhat remodeled, is still in use.

56. Walter J. Travis. When the Garden City Golf Club was incorporated in 1899, one of its charter members was an Australian-born golf enthusiast, Walter J. Travis, who immediately made a name for himself and the Club by first winning the National Amateur Championships in 1900, 1901 and 1903, then going on to win the coveted British Amateur Championship in 1904 (the year in which he autographed this photo), in addition to repeatedly winning the Garden City Golf Club Championships, the Metropolitan Amateur Championships and the Spring Invitation Tournaments. He became a legend in the world of golf and the pride of the Club. The Spring Invitation Tournament has been renamed the Walter J. Travis Memorial Tournament. A room in the clubhouse has also been named for him, and a portrait and plaque have recently been added.

38   The Garden City Company

57. The Garden City Gun Club, c. 1894. Nicholl Floyd, Jr., Dudley B. Fuller and a teammate are here seen practicing for an important Saturday interclub sweepstakes match. The gun club was founded in 1894, and a small wooden clubhouse was built just east of the great well on 11th Street, its grounds and traps wired with electricity for clay-bird shooting. Charter members took great pride in the little building, whose interior, according to the *Brooklyn Eagle*, "was nicely arranged—with walls hung with suitable portraits and paintings, each of which is framed with the spent cartridges fired by various members of the club on these grounds." Even after the Carteret Gun Club for live-pigeon shooting was established, the Club carried on for a few years before moving to an area further east.

58. The Carteret Gun Club, c. 1897. By 1897 many members of the Garden City Gun Club had come to consider the club too modest, old-fashioned and limited. These members joined the "aristocratic" Carteret Gun Club of New Jersey "for the purpose of laying out a pigeon-shooting plant that would eclipse . . . anything heretofore attempted." High exposed land east of the new golf links was leased from the Garden City Company for this new project, and Richard Howland Hunt was commissioned to design the clubhouse. Unusual in shape, it featured an octagonal central section for lounge and bar, and two wings, one for the gun room and keeper's box and the other for dressing rooms and kennels for the three retrievers. Coops and self-setting traps, giving promise of the "fastest grounds in America," were to face the clubhouse, making it possible for admiring onlookers to watch the sportsmen through the plate-glass windows of the "Ladies' Parlor." A nine-foot fence encircled the entire grounds. The sport proved highly successful; but after a few seasons, despite the high fence, the noise and the sight of wounded birds on lawns and porches forced the club to move east to open land near the Meadow Brook Club. Today the building is used by the County as a senior citizens' center and stands in what is now Eisenhower Park.

59

59. Lake Cornelia/Hubbell's Pond. Titled "Lake, looking East" in handwriting, this early photograph shows manmade Lake Cornelia (named in honor of Mrs. Stewart) as it appeared in 1885. The recently completed Cathedral, at the right, is balanced by the stately Victorian hotel at the left. Between them, the railroad station, stores, Estate office and houses can be glimpsed. The borders of the lake itself are sadly bare, although it had been laboriously dug ten years before in an effort to "beautify the area around the hotel." It was not until the Garden City Golf Club was developed in 1899 that George Hubbell set about landscaping its shores. It is now a beautiful lake, with residences on its west banks and the golf club to the east. (It also provides a water hazard for the eighteenth hole.) In the early days, ice from the lake was cut and stored; today the club allows the public to use it for skating.

60. The Garden City Station, c. 1898. In 1898 transportation to Garden City was still largely by train, but the guests attracted by the popular new hotel and clubs were finding the old mansard-roofed station (see no. 17) small and inconvenient. As a result of George Hubbell's previous connection with the L.I.R.R., a new low brick station was built, complete with a "suitable covered driveway, where passengers could enter carriages without being exposed to rain and storms." Even more important, it was provided with a large baggage wing for boxes, steamer trunks, bicycles and golf and polo gear. Located in the large, shrubbery-filled park, with a fountain playing nearby, and across from the hotel, it was considered the "finest station on the road." The station is still in use today.

61. A Canopy-Top Surrey. "Bert Totten at the reins" is the caption written below this 1890s photograph. A horsedrawn canopy-top surrey of this type was evidently a common sight on the treelined avenues, waiting at the railroad station or turning into the hotel driveway. The solid panel body was usually painted black with suitable striping or ornamentation, the gears were dark green with gold stripe, and the full fringe on the top was nicely trimmed. The double surrey harness, with bridles, collars, hams, bellybands, traces and lines, looks complicated, but the big stable on 7th Street had a well-stocked harness room where it could have been purchased, and could have provided the handsome horses as well. The broad avenue in the background might be almost any one of the village's many beautiful roads.

The Garden City Company 41

62. The Hotel Fire, 1899. On September 17, 1899, early in the morning, Mr. Hubbell's newfangled telephone rang to report that Garden City's beautiful new hotel (see no. 50) was burning. According to the *New York Times*, the fire was well out of hand before the local fire brigade and those of neighboring villages had arrived. Fortunately, the guests had been evacuated. The firemen with their hoses stormed the porches and front entrances. Furniture and valuables were carried out, and smaller objects, including books and the hotel register, were tossed out of windows. There was still time for the café and wine cellars to be emptied, and soon eager volunteers were at work—many availing themselves of this unusual opportunity to sample the hotel's stock. The sheriff was called, order was soon restored and the crowd dispersed before the cupola fell, leaving only the blackened porches and brick shell of the central section. Stanford White's distinguished creation had lasted only four years. The only comfort was that no one was injured and that insurance would cover the damage.

THE TURN OF THE CENTURY

63. The Nassau County Court House. In 1899 the Garden City Company had to change the address on its letterhead from "Queens County" to "Nassau County"; and since a new county needed a new courthouse, Hicksville, Hempstead and Mineola were soon vying for the prize. Ever farsighted, the Company offered a five-acre site within Garden City's borders, ideally located near the L.I.R.R.'s main line on the corner of Old Country Road and Franklin Avenue. The offer was accepted, the courthouse was built, and, although it was always thereafter referred to as the Mineola Court House, Garden City had the satisfaction of having made an important gift to the new County. Designed by William Tubby in the Neo-Palladian Classical Revival style, it is a handsome one-story, rectangular building of poured concrete with moulded stucco walls, built at a cost of $300,000. A central rotunda supports a gilded dome, which itself is crowned with a delightful Victorian lacy cast-iron tiara. The County seal is emblazoned over the front entrance, and within, at that time, were housed the courts, jail, boardrooms and service departments. The cornerstone was laid on July 13, 1900, by Governor Theodore Roosevelt—a great celebration attended by VIPs of the three Townships and a good number of Nassau County's 55,000 residents. The building, which subsequently achieved landmark status, is now used as Nassau County's data-processing center.

64

65

44 *The Turn of the Century*

64. Laying the Cornerstone of the County Court House, 1900. According to the *South Side Observer*, "On Friday last [July 13, 1900] the cornerstone of Nassau County Court House at Mineola was laid by Governor Theodore Roosevelt, and the occasion was fittingly celebrated." This well-attended celebration, as seen above, was held on the flat, bare five-acre site at the corner of Old Country Road (trees and houses upper right) and Franklin Avenue. Sitting with Governor Roosevelt on the large flag-draped platform are such dignitaries as Frederick Hicks, Congressman Townsend Scudder, Colonel William Youngs and Supervisors William Jones and Edwin Willets, to name a few. "Upon the front of the platform," to quote the *Observer* again, "was a large crayon drawing representing the Court House as it was to appear when completed. The cornerstone was suspended by means of a three-legged derrick above its final resting place at the northeast corner of the building." In the immediate foreground are members of one of the bands, their instruments at the ready.

65. The Trolley. A new county with a new courthouse deserved a new means of transportation. In 1901, the Mineola, Hempstead and Freeport Traction Company won the franchise to run a line south from the courthouse through Garden City on Franklin Avenue, as part of a network of trolley lines for Nassau County. This handsome trolley car has just crossed the tracks of the Central Railroad and is headed south on its run to Hempstead. The sign over a dirt road shows the way to the carpenter and blacksmith shops, which were housed in a barnlike brick building near the branch-line railroad tracks. This north–south trolley line was a success from the start, carrying passengers to and from the fairgrounds, the Court House and the south shore and to connections with other lines. It earmarked Franklin Avenue as Garden City's most important thoroughfare.

66. The Restored Hotel. After the disastrous fire of 1899 (see no. 62), the firm of McKim, Mead & White was immediately commissioned to design a larger version of the damaged hotel, with two more wings. Completed in 1901, this beautiful Georgian Revival building became famous for its architecture and widely popular. The cupola that crowned the central section, inspired by that of Independence Hall in Philadelphia, was particularly successful in scale and detail. Within a few years, a ballroom and two transverse wings were to be added, completing the building that was, from the first, the pride of Garden City. (The renovated hotel was finally razed in 1973.) This view, taken from the Cathedral tower, shows the hotel in the ideal setting of its landscaped park. In the immediate foreground are the roof of the Casino and its tennis courts. Also in the foreground are the railroad tracks, the station (with a horse and carriage waiting) and the Estate building (which would be destroyed by fire in 1911), and to the right can be seen the roof and cupola of an "Apostle" house. Well beyond and to the left of the hotel are the waterworks and the domed County Court House. The Manhasset hills form the horizon.

The Turn of the Century 45

67. The Hotel Porches, 1905. These ladies, wearing hats to protect their complexions, are enjoying the wide, sunny porches of the hotel. At this time it was achieving an added popularity as a family resort—a luxurious, comfortable and well-run establishment where children were welcome and privacy was respected. The architects had provided convenient suites, a hundred bathrooms, intimate lounges, a children's dining room and an attic playroom. The hotel park, too, was a perfect playground for guests of any age, with its winding paths, fountains, wooded areas and well-kept croquet lawns. For indoor recreation, a Roman marble swimming pool with shower and needle baths had been built in the basement.

68. Cab Service, 1907. The Garden City Hotel in 1907 was probably enjoying its finest hour. Ever since the first Vanderbilt Cup Race in 1904, it had been patronized by "Willie K" Vanderbilt and his wealthy friends (see nos. 70–72). Other prominent, important and even internationally known guests were staying at the hotel for polo matches at Meadow Brook, tournaments at the Garden City Golf Club, races at Belmont or the large and fashionable parties in the hotel ballroom. Since the automobile was all but replacing the horse and carriage, the Garden City Company had built a large garage on 7th Street to encourage the trend. In addition, it had established a fleet of identical chauffeur-driven cabs that could be rented for an hour, a day, a week or longer. Here we see five of these charming conveyances, engines running, waiting to pick up their passengers.

69. The Garden City Garage. During the first three years of the Vanderbilt Cup Races, the village had the problem of finding shelter for the large, valuable foreign and American racing cars that were competing. Sheds were hastily built next to the stable on 7th Street; a Mercedes was eased into George L. Hubbell's barn, a Panhard into the Baldwins' stable, a Pope Toledo into the Townsends'. Now Vanderbilt was about to build a motor parkway with an access tollhouse off Clinton Road, and conservative touring cars driven by chauffeurs were bringing guests to the hotel. The automobile age had arrived, and the Garden City Company welcomed it, in 1907, by building this large brick, steel and cement garage on the corner of Franklin Avenue and 7th Street. It housed sixty cars and provided a repair and machine shop as well. Although the Cup Races ended in 1910, the garage was to simplify the transition from the horse and carriage to the automobile for both residents and hotel guests. In 1920, two World War I pilots, George and Gerard Hughes, bought the garage and ran it successfully for the next thirty years. It was later torn down and replaced by a Texaco station.

70. William K. Vanderbilt, Jr. In October 1904, not only the American Packard but Fiat, Renault, Panhard and Mercedes racing cars were raising clouds of dust on Garden City roads and avenues. These foreign cars, accompanied by the finest drivers of Europe, had arrived on Long Island to compete in the 284.4-mile, closed-circuit Vanderbilt Cup Race. The event had been conceived and sponsored by William K. Vanderbilt, Jr., the millionaire sportsman, to encourage organized international racing in the United States and to prod American car manufacturers to improve the domestic product. He had also donated a 10½-gallon silver cup designed by Tiffany. According to the *Times*, "the famed Garden City Hotel now became the headquarters of the A.A.A. Racing Board, and from this delightful center poured all news and propaganda of the great race." This was held on October 8 on a course roughly encircling Garden City by means of turnpikes and cross roads, and was won by a ninety-horsepower French Panhard. The course was to vary each subsequent year, and delighted crowds were to grow larger and more uncontrolled. In 1910 the State Legislature prohibited automobile racing on public roads and highways. But in 1908 an American driver in an American-built auto won "The Classic," ending the supremacy of the foreign car.

71. Vanderbilt Cup Race, 1906. Photographer William Pickering caught No. 8 bouncing over a railroad crossing during the third Vanderbilt Cup Race as Ralph Peters of Garden City, president of the L.I.R.R., watched with his guests from the rear platform of his private car. Although the front wheels of No. 8 suggest speed, the racing car had been slowed down 100 yards before the crossing by the required green warning banner and is actually just managing to keep in motion. These checkpoints, where the crowds could get a close look at car and driver, were the most popular spots on the course. Enthusiastic about any form of transportation, Peters was to encourage the development of the automobile, and later the airplane, which was to play an important role at Garden City's two airfields. His large home, designed by Aymar Embury, was built on the former site of the Carteret Gun Club, now called Carteret Place. Overlooking the golf course, it is still one of the handsomest residences in the village.

72. Vanderbilt Cup Race, 1908. This photograph, taken October 24, 1908, before the fourth Vanderbilt Cup Race was to begin, shows Vanderbilt himself, as starter and referee, at the far left. Next to him is Chairman Thompson talking to 23-year-old George Robertson, goggles and mask in place, at the wheel of his large 120-horsepower Locomobile No. 16, while his mechanic straps on a spare tire. In the background is the crowded grandstand, decorated for the occasion, on Jericho Turnpike, where the ten-lap Cup Races always started and ended. Several hours and 284 miles later, at this same spot, shouts of "Car coming!" were to give way to a great roar from the crowd as Vanderbilt, the checkered flag, Robertson and the Locomobile merged momentarily in a cloud of dust at the finish line. As one jubilant reporter wrote, "The Cup is America's at last; the supremacy of the foreign car has ended; an American-built car has won 'The Classic.' " The famous Locomobile is now owned by Peter Helck, author of *The Checkered Flag*.

73. The Gold Bug Hotel, 1909. In 1909 this unlikely saloon and boarding house on Old Country Road near the Mineola railroad station became headquarters for the N. Y. Aeronautic Society. Its members had just bought Glenn Curtiss's *Golden Flyer*, affectionately known as the "Gold Bug," and needed "a nice flat place" to try it out. In a two-pole circus tent nearby, the "first American-built plane to be commissioned" was assembled and then pushed across Old Country Road onto a big stubbly field east of Washington Avenue and the carriage sheds of the county fairgrounds. The Society had leased this ideal treeless area from the Garden City Company, which was delighted to encourage the new sport. Experimental planes of all sorts appeared daily, and on-the-spot sheds, hangars and a grandstand were quickly erected. Fencing was installed along Washington Avenue to enclose the pioneer airstrip. Unknowingly, these young aspiring aeronauts had established the first organized airfield on Long Island, which was to be famous for the next four years as the Washington Avenue (or Mineola) Field. In 1912 all aviation activities were moved further east beyond Clinton Road.

74. Glenn Hammond Curtiss, 1909. Hands on the controls, Glenn Hammond Curtiss is seated in the forward-protruding seat of the *Golden Flyer*; the radiator grill of the four-cylinder, twenty-horsepower motor and its propeller are at his back. Clamped around his upper arms is the shoulder yoke that controls the ailerons of his Herring/Curtiss pusher plane. This photograph was probably taken soon after he had won the Scientific American Trophy at that "fine field for flying near Mineola" on July 17, 1909. To quote further from his own account in *The Curtiss Aviation Book:* "The weather was perfect and everything worked smoothly. I made twelve circuits of the course, which completed the twenty-five kilometers, in thirty-two minutes . . . . Great was the enthusiasm of the crowd when the flight ended. I confess that I, too, was enthusiastic over the way the motor worked and the ease with which the machine could be handled in flight." Eight years later, at the start of World War I, Curtiss was back in Garden City at the Curtiss Aeroplane and Motor Corporation designing and building four trimotor hydroplanes for the Navy, one of which, the NC-4, was to succeed in crossing the Atlantic Ocean (see no. 114).

50   The Turn of the Century

75. The Washington Avenue Airfield, 1909. Here we see Glenn Curtiss flying the "Gold Bug" around the triangular course at the Washington Avenue Field, where he will try for the Scientific American Trophy. One of the makeshift pylon markers can be seen at the left, its flag drooping. In the background are the roofs of the carriage sheds that fenced in the well-kept county fairgrounds (now the Nassau County court complex). The group of awed onlookers seems to be standing trustfully in the middle of the course (now the site of Bayberry Street and Fair Court, east of Washington Avenue). A year later, this airfield was to become the headquarters for aviators and flying enthusiasts from all over. A grandstand was built, and flying schools were started. Records were broken at the field; distance flights were inaugurated there. And even in these early days, the sport was being pursued by both sexes, as the *Hempstead Sentinel* reported: "At the airport east of the Garden City Hotel women aviators were active. Miss Scott was out in Captain Baldwin's plane. Miss Moisant drove a monoplane and Miss Bessie Raiche, who is working on a model of her own design, was among others [doing the same]."

76

77

76. The First Public-School Building. This one-story, red-brick, white-trimmed schoolhouse was built in 1902 at the end of 7th Street and Cathedral Avenue on land bought from the Garden City Company. Up to that time, grammar-school classes had been held in a large room over Poole's general store on Hilton Avenue as part of Hempstead's School District No. 1 (see nos. 28 and 29). In 1885 the village achieved its own district by Act of Legislature, and assumed responsibility for public education in the growing village. When school opened in 1902, a Mrs. Taft was in charge and George L. Hubbell was president of the school board. By 1907, a Mrs. Bishop, with a staff of four, was responsible for over one hundred students (kindergarten through grade six). In 1911 the school budget, raised by tax levy, peaked at $6000, and plans for building a second story were under way. The attractive two-story structure is now used as the school district's administration building.

77. A "Little School" Classroom, c. 1905. Inside the school, the students sat with folded hands in orderly rows, the wall clock well behind them, waiting patiently for class to begin. In later years, children commuting from the newly developed Garden City Estates section used the unreliable 8:31 train as an excuse for late arrival.

78. The Firehouse, 1909. Although the village fire department was still managing with a horsedrawn hook-and-ladder truck and a few handdrawn hose carts in 1909, the Garden City Company built this sturdy two-story brick firehouse on the south side of 7th Street. The lower floor, with its wide door, housed the apparatus, which was soon to include the first motor-driven combination Kelly Springfield hose and chemical truck. The upper floor provided office space, as well as quarters and room for general expansion for the department. In 1919 these quarters were taken over by the newly incorporated village as a temporary Village Hall until the stable and carriage house next door could be completely remodeled for that purpose (see nos. 15 and 118). The current Village Hall and firehouse are now on Stewart Avenue; the old firehouse was razed to make way for the commercial development of 7th Street.

The Turn of the Century

79. The Salisbury Links Clubhouse, 1907. Golf was fast becoming a popular sport, and the guests at the hotel had no course on which to play. In 1907, to meet this pressing need, the Garden City Company opened the Salisbury Links, an eighteen-hole golf course of 6000 yards, to be operated as a public subscription course open to all approved players, ladies as well as men. These well-maintained links soon rivaled the Garden City Golf Club in popularity. Walter F. Travis, who laid out the course, stated that "the most striking feature of the course is the provision for all classes of players, from the very top-notcher to the veriest duffer . . . it furnishes the best test of golf that is to be found on this side [of the Atlantic]."

The attractive clubhouse had porches overlooking the fairways and contained lockers, baths and parlors, with an entrance for the exclusive use of the ladies. The Salisbury Links soon absorbed the members of the Midland Golf Club (founded in 1899), which had lost its nine-hole course south of 4th Street to the real-estate plans of the Garden City Company. Salisbury was operated as a community golf club until 1916, when it reincorporated as a private club and changed its name to the Cherry Valley Golf Club.

GARDEN CITY ESTATES

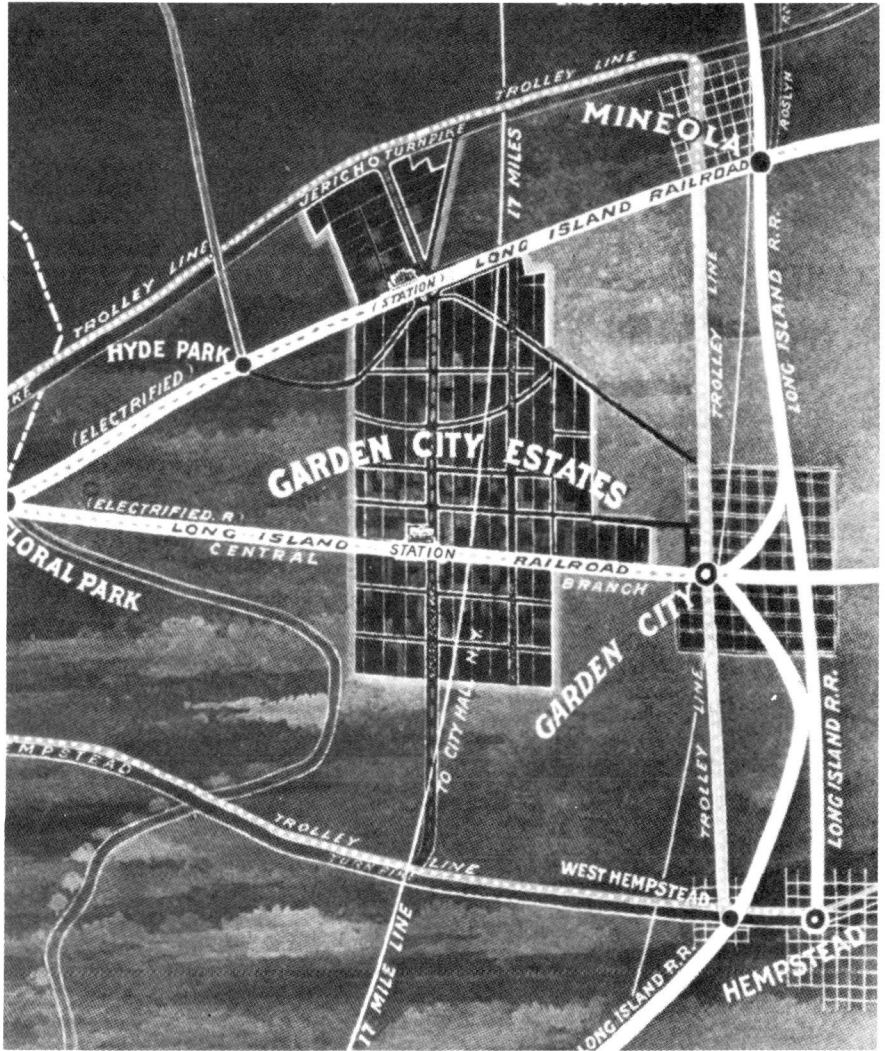

80. Garden City Estates, 1907. This free-style map, from a 1907 promotional booklet of the Garden City Estates Corporation, shows the plans made for the development of the square-mile tract purchased in 1906 from the Garden City Company for $1,500,000. Located between West Hempstead and the main line of the L.I.R.R., its boundary on the west was to be Tanner's Pond Road; on the east, Westminster Road and old Garden City. Available transportation to the new community is emphasized. Founded and funded by a syndicate of wealthy New York businessmen, with standards as high and lavish as those of A. T. Stewart, the Corporation had engaged Cyril E. Marshall and Charles Leavitt, Jr., prominent civil engineers, to produce the master plan. The architectural firm of Kirby, Petit & Green was to design the station and landscaping, and a specially organized construction company was formed to build the suburb of Garden City Estates. Gage E. Tarbell of the Equitable Life Assurance Society was named president and former Lieutenant Governor Timothy L. Woodruff vice president. Today's map of the Estates section is much the same, but this community, founded and run as a separate incorporated entity for twelve years, has been since 1919 an integral part of the Village of Garden City.

81. Building Nassau Boulevard, 1906. For this photograph, over thirty workmen have taken a break from their job of building Nassau Boulevard, which was to be the important north–south avenue through Garden City Estates. Typical of road construction of that day are the heavy wagons drawn by pairs of workhorses and the workmen's garb of overalls, baggy trousers, cotton shirts and sun hats. In contrast to the horse-drawn wagons is one of the new steam-driven road-building machines that were to replace the slow, backbreaking manual labor of the past. The boulevard was to link the community to West Hempstead on the south, run north as far as the main line of the L.I.R.R., and at midpoint cross the Central Railroad, where the Garden City Estates station was to be built.

82. The Gage Tarbell House. This impressive house on Stewart Avenue was built in 1908 by Gage E. Tarbell, president of the Garden City Estates, on a full block between Nassau Boulevard and Euston Road "to show his confidence in the new community." Vice president of the Equitable Life Assurance Society, he, with other wealthy New York businessmen, had founded the Estates Corporation to develop the empty tract of land purchased from the Garden City Company. His standards in carrying out every aspect of the enterprise were so high that the Garden City Company asked him to develop the eastern section of the village in 1910. This house was designed by Oswald Hering, noted for his use of stucco and concrete. Distinctive features were the tapestry tiles used on the roof, the classical entrance door and the sun-rooms at either end. In 1918 Tarbell sold the property to Glenn Curtiss, head of the Curtiss Engineering Company. No trace of this large estate remains; the Unitarian Church has replaced the house, and residences have been built on the other three sides of the block.

83. Garden City Estates Station and Plaza, 1908. This photograph shows several features of the new development: the $10,000 brick railroad station with a cupola; the brick-paved access plaza behind it; the landscaped park, with its pergola, stretching north to Stewart Avenue; the unusual divided boulevard with curbs and sidewalks. South of this bandbox station plaza are the newly built houses conforming to the Garden City Estates' stipulation of "no flat or mansard roofs." The meticulous landscaping was done by A. R. Petit, who was to be responsible for the lavish planting throughout the community. Today the park has been replaced by residences, Nassau Boulevard has been widened and the central dividers have been narrowed. The station, the handsomest in Garden City, remains in use.

84

85

58 Garden City Estates

84. The Estates Clubhouse, 1908. To provide a social club similar to the Casino, the Garden City Estates Corporation built a large, two-story clubhouse on North Road east of the station plaza on a generously landscaped site. To quote from the June 1911 issue of *Country Life in America:* "Frankly, the clubhouse at Garden City Estates is distinctive. Every resident belongs. The freedom of the clubhouse is yours—the parlor, reading room, café, and the comprehensive facilities for impromptu entertainment, indoors and out. After all, what can beat a good game of tennis on a perfect court; and our courts are the meeting place for all tennis enthusiasts from 'round about." According to Ernest Marshall, son of engineer Cyril Marshall, who had laid out the streets of Garden City Estates, he and his brother "went to Sunday School in the clubhouse, and in the afternoon all the residents collected to watch the 'top-notchers' stage an exhibition match." The clubhouse flourished until the larger and even more "distinctive" Garden City Country Club, with its golf course, was built in 1916 (see no. 87).

85. The Stable-Garage, 1908. "The stable-garage was an important place for my brother and me because of Denver, the pony," wrote Ernest Marshall. Marshall's story, *Growing Up in Garden City Estates*, goes on to describe this large, two-story stucco building on Cambridge Avenue, which "used to accommodate a dozen horses and as many wagons and carriages on one side, and automobiles on the other. The second floor housed the stablemen and their families." The stable, he relates, also housed the "team of horses for the horse-drawn ladder truck which the volunteer fire department, Garden City Estates Hose Company, used along with their two-wheeled hose cart." As time went on, automobiles took over, the building was razed and residences were built on the site.

86. The Electric Train, 1908. As this electric train makes one of its first runs on the Hempstead Branch of the L.I.R.R., one can just glimpse an old-fashioned horsedrawn carriage behind the station. This enthusiastic group will ride in the clean, smokeless train to Flatbush Avenue in Brooklyn, where they will take the subway to Manhattan. Two years later, their train will take them through the tunnel under the East River to Pennsylvania Station at 34th Street. (Notice the covered third rail running parallel to the tracks.)

87. The Garden City Country Club, 1916. Garden City Estates, under the leadership of Gage Tarbell, founded the Garden City Country Club in 1916. Its large, welcoming clubhouse, built on Stewart Avenue west of Nassau Boulevard, dominated a rolling sweep of still-undeveloped plainland to the southwest. The challenging course, most of which was south of the railroad tracks, was designed by Walter J. Travis (see no. 56), who had already laid out the Salisbury (Cherry Valley) course. Two years later, when Tarbell resigned as president of the club, its members wrote in gratitude for his efforts, "As a result this complete club house overlooks a complete golf course where two years ago only wild weeds and grass grew." This popular private club, along with the Cherry Valley and Garden City Golf Clubs, have enriched the village with hundreds of acres of unspoiled open land—unusual for a village so near New York.

88. The Timothy Woodruff House on Stewart Avenue, 1908. A founder and vice president of the Garden City Estates Corporation, former Lieutenant Governor Timothy L. Woodruff built his large Dutch Colonial home east of Nassau Boulevard on Stewart Avenue, which had been extended to the west in 1880 when St. Paul's School was being constructed. Enthusiastic, social and sports-loving, he sponsored the community clubhouse for tennis, shared the excitement of the ongoing Vanderbilt Cup Races, and became deeply involved with the early aviation activities of the N. Y. Aero Club at the Washington Avenue Field. By 1910, president of both Garden City Estates and the Aero Club, he developed the sophisticated Nassau Boulevard Aerodrome in order to encourage aviation, promote flying schools and host the second International Aviation Meet. His contacts and influence were also of use in acquiring authorization for the first airmail flight from the field in 1911.

89. International Aviation Meet Pennant, 1911. This colorful felt banner, depicting a symbolic winged propeller, a variety of airplanes and even a cloud or two, was a popular souvenir at the International Aviation Meet held in 1911 at the Nassau Boulevard Aerodrome. This well-equipped field, located west of Roxbury Road and Nassau Boulevard in the undeveloped northwest section of the new community, and headquarters of the Aero Club of New York, proved to be an ideal site for the weeklong (Sept. 23–Oct. 1) competitive event. It had easy access by rail, grounds of over 350 acres, many hangars and grandstands. Thousands of spectators arrived by train or automobile. Famous aviators were present, piloting airplanes of all sorts. The first airmail flight was made. But such continued aerial activity was not conducive to suburban growth. The field, along with the Washington Avenue field, was moved a year later to the open plainland east of Clinton Road. This larger airfield was incorporated as the Hempstead Plains Aerodrome and became Hazelhurst Field at the start of the World War (see nos. 104 and 108).

90. Postmaster General Hitchcock and Earle Ovington, 1911. Postmaster General Frank H. Hitchcock has just handed a locked sack of airmail to Earle Ovington, Airmail Pilot No. 1, who is sitting in his Blériot "Queen Monoplane" at the Nassau Boulevard Aerodrome, ready to take off for the Mineola post office. Hitchcock seems pleased with the successful mail-by-air postal service he has inaugurated in cooperation with Timothy Woodruff, general manager of this second International Aviation Meet. Ovington seems equally pleased. The airmail flights, challenging and crowd-pleasing, have still left him enough time to enter the scheduled aerial events along with the thirty-six men and women flyers from various countries who are also competing. He himself had learned to fly in Paris, and is seen wearing his favorite French helmet. This site in the Estates section is now a residential area.

91. The First Airmail Flight, Sept. 23, 1911. This drawing depicts Earle Ovington in his Blériot monoplane No. 13, his sack of mail between his knees. He is leaving the Nassau Boulevard Aerodrome to deliver the mail to the Mineola post office. At the lower right is the large canvas tent known as U.S. Mail Aeroplane Station No. 1, where he has just picked up the sack of letters and postcards stamped by Postal Inspector Boyle. To the rear are the small hangars, their flags flying, which lined Roxbury Road; each bears the name of a competing flyer in the second International Aviation Meet. (Out of sight are the grandstands, box seats, admission booths, judges' stand, private automobile boxes and vendors' booths.) In the middle distance a "pusher" biplane is flying near the crowd of over 20,000, gathered to watch such scheduled aerial events as a cross-country race, speed and relay races, women's altitude contests, aerial scouting and passenger biplane flights. The airmail flight had not been listed in the program.

GARDEN CITY EAST

92

93

94

92. The Garden City Company Office, 1912. In 1910 the success of Garden City Estates prompted the Garden City Company to "develop the tract of 640 acres lying east of the Garden City Hotel and to make improvements on a scale heretofore unattempted." The area stretched from Franklin Avenue to Clinton Road, and from Old Country Road to Meadow Street. When the company's former "Estate building" northwest of the railroad station (see no. 20) was gutted by fire, plans were quickly made for a larger and more modern office building. This handsome structure, located northeast of the station, looks more like a small museum, but it provided ideal accommodations for the engineers, architects and company staff who were planning and designing this important new development. Gage Tarbell was put in charge, and the engineering firm of Cyril E. Marshall and Charles Leavitt, Jr., was used once more. This dignified building served the company for the next forty-four years until, in 1956, it was deeded to the village as a public library. Although the two-story Hubbell Wing was added soon afterwards, the building was reluctantly razed in 1973 to make room for a larger, more easily staffed library building.

93. Subdivision East, Stewart Avenue. True to the promise in this architect's rendering, the Stewart Avenue Mall leading from Franklin Avenue through Garden City East to Clinton Road was to become one of the most beautiful avenues on Long Island (see also no. 88). Planned on a lavish scale, it is 180 feet wide; the two roadways enclose a parklike central mall, and six rows of specimen trees create a remarkable and stately vista even now. Mrs. Stewart's heirs, through the Garden City Company, invested heavily in developing this rather barren section of Garden City, trusting largely in the prestige lent by the Cathedral, the improved transportation from Pennsylvania Station in New York and the growing popularity of the automobile. Now that roadracing was banned, William K. Vanderbilt was promoting his Long Island Motor Parkway to Ronkonkoma, with Garden City's access tollhouse on Clinton Road the important entrance. Stewart Avenue was to be the link from the village, with its beautiful hotel and new garage, to eastern Long Island, with its further attractions for the tourist. The personal involvement of the heirs in this venture accounts for the family names of the streets leading from the mall: Butler, Devereux, Wetherill, Emmet, Osborne, Lefferts and Huntington.

94. The Clinton Road Station, c. 1910. The Clinton Road railroad station, built for the newly developed eastern section of Garden City, was served from the start by a trolley car instead of a train. Since few houses had been built at that time, a shuttle trolley car, "equipped with third-rail shoes and its pole removed," was adequate to transport passengers to and from the Garden City station. During World War I, the little depot played a new role as telegraph and paymaster station for the soldiers at Camp Mills, which had suddenly been established right across the tracks (see no. 110). Freight for the camp passed it by on the way to warehouses (along what is now Commercial Avenue), and the shuttle lent its small services to the "boys" at five cents a ride. After the war, the shuttle stopped at the station on its run to the polo matches at Meadow Brook and the golf at Salisbury (now Eisenhower) Park. In World War II, a more sophisticated two-car passenger train carried thousands of servicemen from Roosevelt and Mitchel Fields to the Country Life Press Station for the New York connection. Later the building served as a substation of the Garden City Fire Department, and it is now used by the village as temporary office space.

Garden City East 63

95

95. The Long Island Motor Parkway. These three Packards are on a newly built nine-mile stretch of the Long Island Motor Parkway, which was to be used for the 1907 Vanderbilt Cup Race if completed in time. Although the two previous races had been spectacular successes, Vanderbilt recognized that, because of the immense crowds of over 200,000, the dangers of roadracing were increasing. To solve this problem, he and his wealthy friends formed a corporation in 1906 to build the Long Island Motor Parkway—a fenced-in, concrete-paved, crossing-free automobile toll road through central Long Island. Within a year, the *Brooklyn Daily Eagle* reported that "the route has been definitely located and the right of way acquired for the entire distance from Garden City to Ronkonkoma." Eventually the 48-mile parkway was finished, at a cost of three million dollars; eleven tollhouses were provided, sixty-five bridges were constructed and a welcoming inn was erected overlooking the lake at Ronkonkoma. But only small sections of the road were ever used in subsequent Cup races, and in 1910 roadracing on public roads was prohibited by the State Legislature. No longer a speedway, the road became highly popular with an enthusiastic public. Although it retained its popularity for many years, the parkway succumbed to competitive modern highways and was closed down in 1937, its right-of-way given to the Long Island Park Commission.

96. The Tollhouse, 1911. This tollhouse is the one remaining lodge of the identical eleven built by Vanderbilt for his Motor Parkway, which by 1911 ran from Hillside Avenue in Queens to Lake Ronkonkoma. In line with the high standards applied to the parkway, he chose an already prominent architect, John Russell Pope, to design these small buildings (as well as the inn overlooking the lake) in French Provincial style. Although more suited to the French countryside than to the Hempstead Plains, they added charm to the winding, landscaped motor road. Built of stuccoed brick and wood, with a tall central chimney and a steeply pitched roof, this small lodge was home to tollkeeper Christian Ernst and his wife for many years. At this location just south of Roosevelt Field, Mr. Ernst could boast that he had "made change for every famous aviator going or coming to the Field." The tollhouse is now a private residence, as is the neighboring Tudor cottage (see no. 97), formerly the office of the parkway's manager. These two buildings, along with a remaining strip of the parkway behind them, form a small historic district called Vanderbilt Court.

97. L. I. Motor Parkway Office. This Tudor cottage, just west of the Garden City tollhouse, was built soon after World War I to replace a temporary wooden building used by A. R. Pardington, first manager of the Motor Parkway, and occasionally by Vanderbilt himself. It stands just east of Clinton Road, where the parkway, after curving through the northeast corner of Garden City, crossed Clinton Road on a steel-and-concrete bridge. The cottage initially served as a central office for the construction and maintenance of the 48-mile toll road, and later, when this new office was built, as a home for a subsequent manager. After the road was closed in 1937, the cottage was rented, then sold as a private residence. A rolltop desk left behind in the basement was found to contain one of Pardington's photo albums depicting the building of the parkway and tollhouses; the album is now in the Garden City archive collection.

96

97

98.

98. Doubleday, Page and Company, 1910. In 1910, with the East River tunnel completed and transportation to Long Island assured, the small publishing house of Doubleday, Page and Company moved its operations to Garden City. After purchasing forty acres on the east side of Franklin Avenue, the company quickly built its all-under-one-roof plant. Designed by the firm of Kirby and Petit "to resemble Hampton Court in England" and surrounded by landscaped gardens, the Country Life Press, as it was called, became a welcome addition to the village. Frank Nelson Doubleday had actively involved himself in this project, as had Walter Hines Page, who came to live at 32 Cathedral Avenue until he was appointed ambassador to Great Britain in 1914. Well-known authors, editors and other people prominent in publishing were to be part of the scene for many years. During World War II, the plant was greatly enlarged and its beautiful gardens were replaced by parking lots; it was completely converted to office space in 1956. Doubleday was sold to the West German firm of Bertelsmann in 1986.

99. Laying the Doubleday Cornerstone, 1910. Straw boaters were in order on August 19, 1910, when ex-President Theodore Roosevelt laid the cornerstone of Country Life Press. Colonel Roosevelt, amid prominent guests, can be seen addressing the large gathering from a low platform, his right hand characteristically outstretched. This ceremony took place in front of the partially constructed building, which was being built in record time. By November the company's 700 employees were producing 6500 books a day—the figure that had been set as their goal. The completed structure would cover more than six acres and house not only the printing and power plants but the executive offices, library, bindery, carpenter shop, storage and shipping rooms and the Western Union and telephone systems as well. Its construction cost $267,649.73.

100. Steam Train at Doubleday Plant. Steam locomotive No. 113 is pictured here on the railroad siding that ran between Doubleday's main building and the annex, making it easy to unload paper and other bookmaking materials and to ship finished books. The siding was connected with the L.I.R.R.'s Garden City, West Hempstead and Valley Stream branch (now abandoned), which ran directly behind the plant. The L.I.R.R. also built the small brick Country Life Press station on the Hempstead branch line at Chestnut Street, well within walking distance. This station was to serve not only the Doubleday plant but the entire eastern section of Garden City.

101

102

68 Garden City East

101. Franklin Court, 1912. When Doubleday, Page and Company built its plant on Franklin Avenue in 1910, the Garden City Company cooperated by constructing a complex of attached and semiattached houses on a triangular piece of land conveniently behind it. The design, by the firm of Ford, Butler and Oliver, is an example of imaginative site use and adherence to an original plan. Twenty-two houses, including those shown here, facing the little entrance park, were built in 1912, the remainder in the twenties. By building the two-story stucco, slate-roofed houses close to the encircling roadway, the planners gave each dwelling its own deep, private, walled-in garden, creating a charm and appeal very like that of a Cotswolds village in England. Franklin Court is now widely admired for its unique plan and beautiful gardens. Many Doubleday people have lived there over the years, and it has also attracted architects, writers, artists, professors and young families. Originally only for rent, the houses are now privately owned and in great demand. (*Nassau County Museum*)

102. 821 Franklin Avenue, 1910. This large, extravagantly designed business/apartment building reflects the Garden City Company's determination in 1910 to develop Franklin Avenue as Garden City's principal business street, and Stewart Avenue, with its treelined mall, as the imposing corridor to its new real-estate venture, Garden City East. Located just north of the intersection of these avenues, the building was accessible from any part of the village and also from Mineola and Hempstead by means of the trolley, whose tracks and poles can be seen in the foreground. The Georgian style of the balanced façade and classical entrance was retained in the marble foyer and staircase inside and in the large apartments with fireplaces on the upper floors. Because of this central location, the post office was soon moved from Poole's Hilton Avenue store and installed in these more suitable quarters. The building was later bought by J. F. Klipp, a pharmacist who operated it as a Medical Arts Center, with Klipp's Pharmacy as its main attraction. A wing added and its ground floor altered, this handsome building is still prominent on Franklin Avenue.

103. St. Joseph's Church. In October 1901, in answer to the growing community's need, the parish of St. Joseph was created and Father James Flynn was designated founding pastor. (Eighty Roman Catholics, constituting the membership of the new parish, had formerly gathered for services in the Stewart Arms—later to become the Casino—or the hotel.) In 1903 a site on the southwest corner of 5th Street and Franklin Avenue was purchased from the Garden City Company for $1000, and this handsome red-brick church was erected, along with the parsonage on its left. But as more Catholics moved to Garden City, the need for larger facilities became urgent. In the spring of 1953 the old building was razed, and by Easter 1956 a larger and more modern church had been completed, to which, through the efforts of Rev. Edward McManus, a parochial school was later added.

104

104. The Hempstead Plains Aerodrome, c. 1912. This photograph shows the main entrance to the Hempstead Plains Aerodrome and its administration building, flying two welcoming flags. One represented the Aero Club of America, the other the Hempstead Plains Aviation Corporation, which had been formed in 1911 with a capital of $50,000 to provide a new aerodrome to replace the two overcrowded airfields in Garden City. Located east of Clinton Road, bounded on the north by Old Country Road and on the south by the parkway, it extended east over 900 acres leased from the Garden City Company. The field was well-fenced along both roads; "Hangar Row," composed of five cement and thirty wooden hangars, ran along Old Country Road, and the four grandstands, seating 1600, and the parking areas were on Clinton Road. The field itself, covered with rough grass, was graded only near the hangars and runways. Seven pylons outlined the five-kilometer course. When the field opened in July 1912, flying schools were immediately set up by Alfred Moisant, Giuseppe Bellanca, Sloane and George Beatty as well as the Aero Club. Pilots were licensed, and planes of every type were tested, improved and flown in the five years following. In 1917, this important and well-equipped airfield was taken over as a training center for Army pilots and renamed Hazelhurst Field (the later Roosevelt Field).

105. The Moisant Aviation School, 1912. Flying schools at the two earlier Garden City fields had been modest affairs, but for Alfred Moisant an aviation school required new hangars and a fleet of seven Moisant-type monoplanes with Anzani and Gnome motors. These are visible inside the concrete hangars that formed the western end of "Hangar Row." The group in the center probably includes Moisant, his two instructors and some of his aspiring young students. The training to be a licensed pilot was rigorous, as these wealthy sportsmen discovered en route to the final test, which was always taken early in the morning. The first pilot license given on the new Hempstead Plains field was to W. Irving Twombly from the Sloane School, who piloted a Deperdussin monoplane. According to the October 1912 issue of *Flying*, "the test occurred at five o'clock in a windless morning and Mr. Twombly gave afterwards a very pleasant breakfast party at the Garden City Hotel."

106. An Aviator, 1913. Standing in front of his Blériot-type monoplane, this serious aviator is holding up a dangling cluster of cups to test the velocity of the wind. (A more sophisticated form of this device, now called an anemometer, is still in use.) At the Aerodrome in 1913, windless early-morning or late-afternoon flights were still required for the beginner, but the wind had become a welcome challenge to the more experienced flyer, lifting him to new heights. Altitude meant colder air, and the flying outfits for men and "birdwomen" became heavier, making use of leather or fleece lining. The outfit seen here was typical—full breeches tucked into puttees, a high-fastened coat, often belted, gauntlet gloves and a snug helmet. The women flyers, or "birdwomen," wore similar costumes—the coat nipped in at the waist or belted, the helmet of soft leather framing the face. Daring Harriet Quimby always wore a long, white, floating scarf as well. As *New Country Life* explained, "her innate spirit of coquetry will not allow her to throw her looks entirely to the winds, even if up in the clouds."

105

106

71

WORLD WAR I

107. Hazelhurst's First Reserve Aero Squadron, 1917. Almost overnight, peacetime Hempstead Plains Aerodrome became military Hazelhurst Field when war was declared on April 6, 1917. Flying schools were shut down, grandstands carted away and the administration building moved and replaced with a long row of barracks on Clinton Road. Along Old Country Road, larger hangars were built for the JN-4D planes—the famous Curtiss "Jenny," which became the basic

108

trainer for thousands of pilots during the war years. By the end of April, fifty young volunteers from Ivy League colleges, among them Quentin Roosevelt, had arrived to form the First Squadron of Reserve Military Aviators. (Thirty-five are in this photograph.) The schedule was heavy, but the young flyers managed to visit Sagamore Hill, estates on the North Shore, Garden City homes and the Garden City Hotel, where they could use the marble swimming pool in the basement. Some, like Quentin Roosevelt (see no. 109), were immediately sent overseas; others first went to other fields as flight instructors; almost all eventually saw service abroad. Hazelhurst was renamed Roosevelt Field when Quentin was killed in 1918, and later Curtiss/Roosevelt. Today it is the site of Roosevelt Shopping Center.

108. Hazelhurst Field, 1917. This rare photograph shows how quickly Hempstead Plains Aerodrome was converted to a military field when the United States entered the war in 1917. In the foreground are the still uncompleted barracks, the mess hall and the administration building, with the supply and repair warehouses beyond. "Hangar Row" is at the rear, along Old Country Road, with the faithful "Jennies" lined up in front. At the right, the field called Hazelhurst I can be seen stretching eastward. Hazelhurst II, used only for a short time, lay to the southeast; its name was soon to be changed to Mitchel Field. The photograph is from the collection of Gerard Hughes, who, with his brother George and Quentin Roosevelt, left Harvard to become an Army pilot here in 1917.

109. Quentin Roosevelt, c. 1917. Youngest of Theodore Roosevelt's six children, Quentin left Harvard when war was declared in April 1917 to become an Army pilot. He received his flight training at Hazelhurst Field and was commissioned first lieutenant in the Aviation Section of the Signal Corps. Ordered overseas, he was sent to Issaudon, France, where he was attached to the 95th Pursuit Squadron. In April 1918, the squadron was sent to the front. Three months later, on July 14, Roosevelt was shot down and killed in aerial combat at the age of 20. Buried by the German army in Chamery, where his plane had crashed, his body was later brought to Colville, Normandy, where his brother, Theodore Roosevelt, Jr., was buried. In his honor, Hazelhurst Field was renamed Roosevelt Field.

109

110. Camp Mills, 1917. This tent city, a camp for thousands of soldiers, actually existed within the borders of Garden City in 1917. For America the war began on April 6, 1917, with the commitment to send troops as well as supplies to Europe. A site near New York City, the embarkation port, was needed at once to mobilize the twenty-seven already trained National Guard regiments into a single division, the Rainbow Division. Garden City, the home of Hazelhurst Field and the Curtiss airplane factory, was the logical choice; transportation, a water supply and a large, flat, undeveloped site to the south on Clinton Road were all available. Named for Brigadier General Albert L. Mills, Camp Mills was bounded on the south by Meadow Street, on the west by Clinton Road, on the north by the Central Railroad and on the east by open plainland (later Mitchel Field). To save time, tents were to be used instead of buildings. Thousands of floorless, four-cot one-polers, easily unrolled and pegged down, were erected as quarters for the troops, and larger tents for all other purposes. This photograph, looking south, shows the indispensable railroad track in the foreground, the supply depot and wagons on a rough road parallel to it (now Commercial Avenue), and beyond, a sea of thousands of tents stretching almost as far as the camera could see.

111. The Rainbow Division Monument. This monument on Clinton Road is in a small park just south of the Clinton railroad station and tracks and opposite Commercial Avenue, which was the entrance to Camp Mills in 1917. It was built and dedicated in 1941 by the veterans of the Rainbow Division in honor of their 2950 dead and 13,290 wounded. On one side of the column, a soldier is depicted standing at attention; a soldier playing his bugle is on another side. Both wear the doughboy uniform of the period—brimmed hat, belted jacket with patch pockets, breeches tucked into rolled leggings and heavy, laced shoes. On the four sides of the base are scenes—one of the tent city, "Camp Albert L. Mills, Birthplace of the Rainbow Division," and three depictions of the fateful battles in France in which the division was involved. The number of soldiers at Camp Mills was overwhelming, but the women of organizations and churches in Hempstead, Garden City and Westbury faithfully staffed the "hostess" and "information" tents, worked in the emergency hospital sheds, gave tea dances and worried about the soldiers. When they left, the proximity of the camp, the sound of taps at night and the many contacts with these young men made it seem as if the division had been Garden City's own.

112. Entrance to Camp Mills, 1918. After the Rainbow Division had departed, the Sunset Division arrived, only to move on to New Jersey when hurricane weather also arrived, blowing down tents and spreading influenza. For a short time the site was deserted; but by early spring more troops were needed to stem an escalating German offensive, and Camp Mills was reactivated—this time as a compact, well-built cantonment, able to accommodate 50,000 troops. The map in the folder given to each soldier shows a pattern of well-marked streets with dry wells, the locations of the 398 barracks, thirty-six officer's quarters, eight lavatories, the administration and mess halls, a laundry, a theater and a library. Directions to the large, 2500-bed hospital on Transverse Road were included. To beautify the camp, trees and shrubs were planted, and near the entrance on Locust Street an attempt was made to outline the stripes of the American flag (foreground). The unexpected armistice in November ended Camp Mills's original role but created a new one, as a major demobilization camp. For at least a year, thousands of troops passed through it on the way home. (*National Archives*)

113. Lieut. William Bradford Turner. Like every community in Long Island, Garden City was completely involved in the war effort, and its young men enlisted in all branches of the armed forces. Six died in the war. One, Lieut. William Bradford Turner, was killed in action on September 27, 1918, while leading an attack against one of the strongest parts of the Hindenburg Line. For bravery on the field of battle, he was posthumously awarded the Congressional Medal of Honor. In Garden City he was honored by its veterans, who in 1919 named their new American Legion post the William Bradford Turner Post.

114.

114. The Curtiss Engineering Plant, 1917. This photograph shows the size of the brick plant hastily constructed in 1917, by Government order, on the east side of Clinton Road just north of the railroad tracks (diagonal right)—the first factory for manufacturing aircraft during World War I. Under Navy auspices, four antisubmarine hydroplanes capable of crossing the Atlantic were to be designed and built by Glenn Hammond Curtiss of Buffalo, established inventor and manufacturer of airplanes (see no. 74). These trimotor flying boats were to be called the NC (Navy/Curtiss) 1, 2, 3 and 4. While the plant was being built, Curtiss drew the master design and had various sections built to specification by other manufacturers. By December he had moved his entire design crew to the Garden City plant. There, sections for all four began to arrive by rail; they were measured, checked and weighed, the wing panels and ailerons were "doped" and finished, and the preliminary assemblage was begun.

115. The NC-4 That Crossed the Atlantic. Although Curtiss's complicated NC operation in Garden City was carried out quickly, the war ended as the ships were being assembled and tested at the Naval Air Base at Rockaway Beach. Even so, the project continued. Three ships started out for Europe on May 8, 1919; the NC-4 arrived safely at Horta, Portugal, on May 17, the only one to cross the Atlantic.

116. Curtiss Aeroplane and Motor Corp. Interior, 1919. The war over and the NC-4 a success, Glenn Hammond Curtiss bought Gage Tarbell's property in the Garden City Estate section (see no. 82) and began "tinkering," as he called it, at his peacetime plant, renamed the Aeroplane and Motor Corporation. There he began turning out a variety of planes for the Army and Navy. His planes broke speed records and won Pulitzer Trophies; he developed the all-metal propeller, and in general gave his genius full play. Among other planes and parts of planes, this photograph shows (center) a tandem-wheeled, trimotor "Eagle"; (left) uncovered wing frames of a "Jenny"; and (right) an "F boat" with its pusher engine and wing-top stabilizers. As a result of the Depression, Curtiss gave up Curtiss Field (the western half of Roosevelt Field) and moved his operations to Valley Stream only a year before he died in 1930. The deserted plant was briefly used for Nassau Collegiate Junior College Center, a state and federal relief program. Rezoned for commercial use in 1947, the buildings were occupied by Sperry Gyroscope for some years, and since then by Esselte Pendaflex.

115

A CRUISE IN
THE NAVY IS A
LIBERAL EDUCATION
APPLY 34 EAST 23RD ST.

116

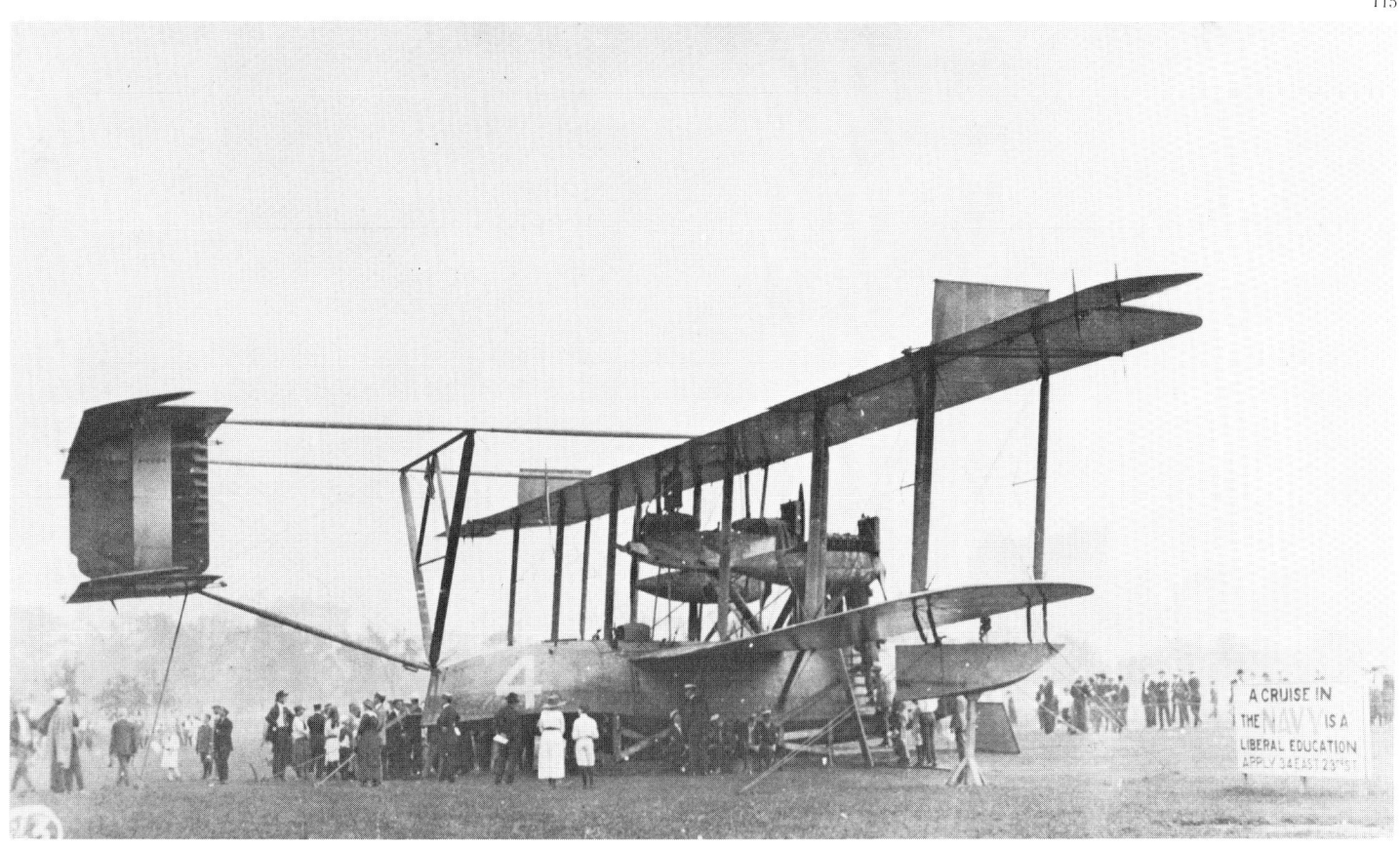

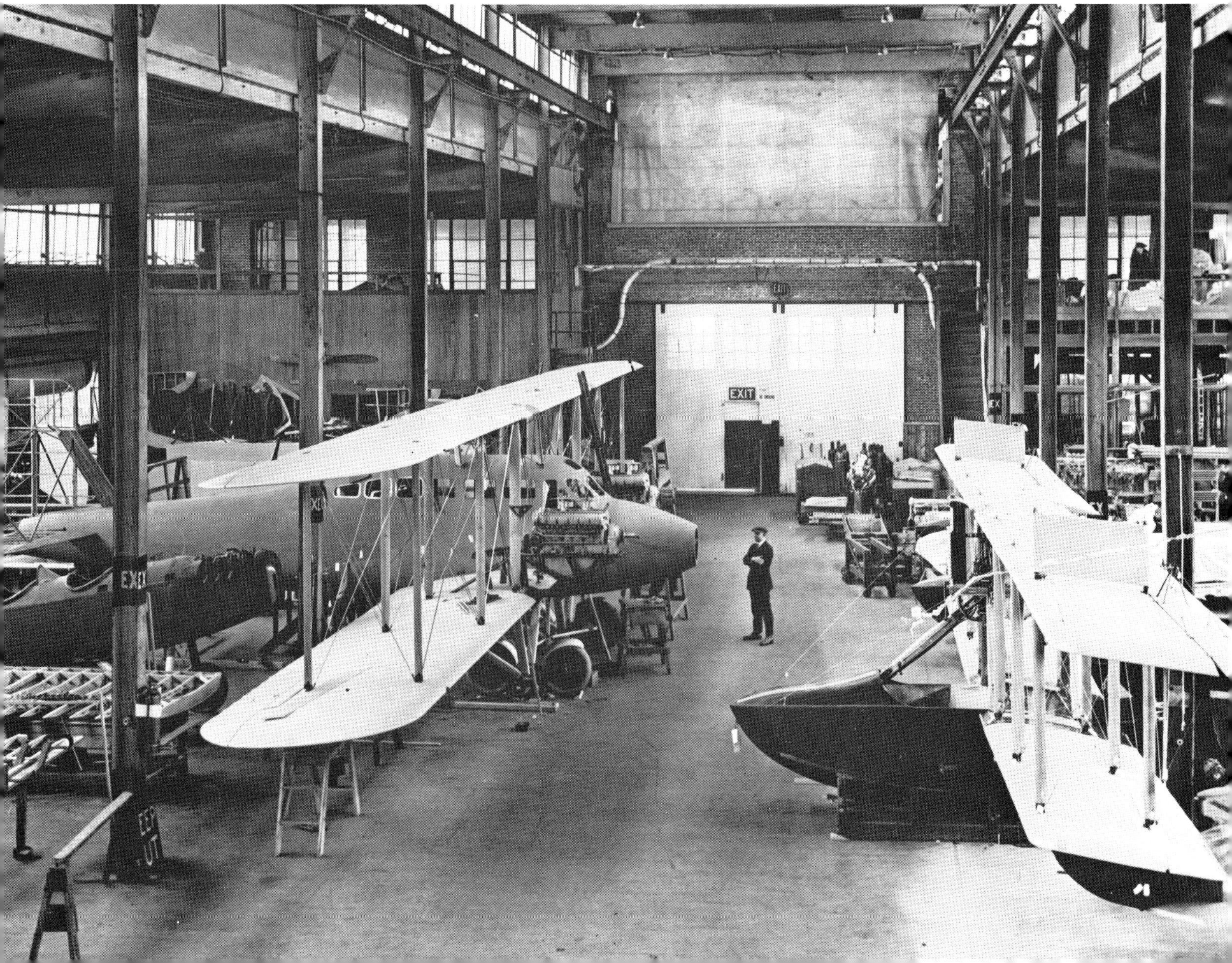
EXIT

117. British Dirigible, 1919. After the war ended in November 1918, competitive efforts to cross the Atlantic by air continued. Less than two months after the NC-4 crossing (no. 115), Britain's R.A.F. rigid airship, the R-34, left Scotland to land at the eastern end of Roosevelt Field on July 6. Here we see this 641-foot-long, hydrogen-filled, silver ship swaying over the heads of a marveling crowd. Its prow is tethered to the ground by a Navy-constructed steel-cable apparatus anchored in cement. It had undergone a 3200-mile, 108-hour flight, complicated by a stowaway, strong winds and high fuel consumption, and ending dramatically with only enough fuel for a few more hours. The landing crew of veterans from Camp Mills had been diverted to Montauk in case of an emergency caused by lack of fuel, but substitutes were hastily found for Roosevelt Field and a safe landing was achieved. To celebrate, the twenty enlisted Royal Navy crew members were taken to Mitchel Field for a specially prepared chicken dinner, and the ten officers to the Garden City Hotel. The dirigible stayed at the field for three days preparing for its successful, and faster, trip back to England. The cargo it had carried to America consisted of films of the Versailles peace treaty, English newspapers and twenty-five pounds of mail.

118. The Village Hall. This photograph shows the Village Hall, flag flying, as the symbol of the end of Garden City's first fifty years and its new status, beginning on May 15, 1919, as the Incorporated Village of Garden City, Hempstead Town, Common School District No. 18 (population 2140). By the end of the war, the three developed sections of Garden City covered almost all of the 5.2 square miles of A. T. Stewart's original master plan. Faced with new challenges and responsibilities, and unwilling to be governed any longer by two private corporations, the residents of the three sections—Garden City Estates, Old Garden City and Garden City East—decided to unite and incorporate under an unusual, nonpolitical form of government called the Community (or Gentlemen's) Agreement, with each section represented on a board of trustees. (By Amendment to the Community Agreement in 1931, Garden City West became the fourth section of the village to be represented on the board.) George L. Hubbell, former manager of the Garden City Company, was the inevitable choice as first mayor. As for this modest, neat building, it is in fact the transformed stable and carriage house on 7th Street that Stewart had built in 1874 (see no. 15). Completely remodeled inside and out, it served in its new capacity until 1953, when a new Village Hall was built on Stewart Avenue. At the far right, the old firehouse (no. 78) can be seen; here, in rooms above the firetruck, village affairs were carried out until the remodeling was done.

BIBLIOGRAPHY

Bassett, Preston R. *Long Island, Cradle of Aviation*. Amityville, N.Y.: Long Island Forum, 1950.

Catalogue of the Stewart Collection. New York: American Art Association, 1887.

Curtiss, Glenn H., and Augustus Post. *The Curtiss Aviation Book*. New York: Frederick A. Stokes Co., 1912.

Denton, Daniel. *Brief Description of New York, Formerly Called New Netherlands, with the Places Thereunto Adjoining*. London, 1670. Reprint, with notes by Gabriel Furman. New York: William Gowans, 1845.

Dwight, Timothy. *Travels in New England and New York*, Vol. 3. New Haven, 1822.

Embury, Aymar. *Country Houses*. New York: Doubleday, Page & Co., 1914.

Floyd-Jones, Thomas. *Backward Glances*. Privately printed, New York, 1914.

Gabriel, Ralph Henry. *The Evolution of Long Island*. New Haven: Yale University Press, 1921.

Garden City News (newspaper), 1923–1963.

Helck, Peter. *The Checkered Flag*. New York: Charles Scribner's Sons, 1961.

History of Queens County, New York. New York: W. W. Munsell, 1882.

Hubbell, George L. Personal scrapbook, 1893–1900. Unpublished. (Garden City Public Library.)

Lessner, Erwin Christian. *Famous Auto Races and Rallies*. New York: Hanover House, 1956.

Lewis, Arnold, James Turner and Steven McQuillin. *The Opulent Interiors of the Gilded Age: All 203 Photographs from "Artistic Houses."* New York: Dover Publications, 1987.

Peters, Ralph. "The Long Island Railroad in the War, 1917–1919." Unpublished typescript. (Garden City Public Library.)

"Posthumous Relatives of the Late Alexander T. Stewart" (Proceedings before the Surrogate Court and excerpts from newspapers, 1876). (New York Public Library.)

Randall, C. Walter. "Garden City: Its Incorporation as a Village and Its Community Agreement." Pamphlet. 1954.

Reifschneider, Felix E. "History of the Long Island Railroad." In Hazelton's *The Boroughs of Brooklyn and Queens, the Counties of Nassau and Suffolk*, Vol. 1, pp. 384–420. New York, 1925.

Resseguie, Harry E. Biography of A. T. Stewart. Unpublished.

_____. "The Decline and Fall of the Commercial Empire of A. T. Stewart." *Harvard Business History Review*, Fall 1962.

Ross, Peter. *A History of Long Island*. New York: Lewis Publishing Co., 1903.

Schoendorf, Robert. *The Pioneer Flights of Garden City Estates, New York, 1911*. New York: Al Zimmer, 1982.

Schultz, Bernice. *Colonial Hempstead*. Lynbrook, N.Y.: Review-Star Press, 1937.

Seyfried, Vincent F. *The Founding of Garden City 1869–1893*. Uniondale, N.Y.: Salisbury Printers, 1969.

_____. *New York and Long Island Traction Company*. Privately printed, 1952.

Shanks, Maj. Gen. David C. *As They Passed Through the Port*. Washington, D.C.: Cary Publishing Co., 1927.

[Sheldon, G. W.] *Artistic Houses*. New York: D. Appleton, 1883–84. Reprint. New York: Benjamin Blom, 1971.

Smith, Louise Carter. "Long Island Motor Parkway." *Nassau County Historical Journal*, Vol. 22 (Spring 1961).

Smith, M. H. *Early History of the Long Island Railroad 1834–1900*. Uniondale, N.Y.: Salisbury Printers, 1958.

_____. *History of Garden City*. Manhasset, N.Y.: Channel Press, 1963. Updated edition. Garden City: Garden City Historical Society, 1980.

Smits, Edward J. *The Creation of Nassau County*. Mineola, N.Y., 1960.

Thompson, Benjamin F. *History of Long Island*. Third edition. New York: Robert H. Dodd, 1918.

Tredwell, Daniel N. *Personal Reminiscences of Men and Things on Long Island*. New York: G. P. Putnam's Sons, 1924.

Walling, George W. *Recollections of a New York Chief of Police*. New York: Caxton Book Concern, 1887.

Youngs, Mary Fanny. "History of the Cathedral of the Incarnation." Unpublished monograph. (Garden City Public Library.)

INDEX

The numbers refer to pages.

A. T. Stewart Era Buildings, 16, 30
Ackley brothers (butchers), 19
Adelphi University, viii
Aero Club of America, 70
Aero Club of New York: *see* New York Aeronautic Society
"Apostle" houses, 6, 14, 16, 21, 29, 30, 45

Beatty, George, 70
Bellanca, Giuseppe, 70
Bishop, Mrs. (schoolteacher), 53
Bishop's Residence, 10, 27, 29
Boyle (postal inspector), 61
Briel, Kitty, 19
Butler, Maxwell, 31

Camp [Albert L.] Mills, viii, 63, 74, 75
Carteret Gun Club, 39, 49
Cathedral of the Incarnation, 10, 14, 21, 23, 25, 27, 29, 30, 33, 37, 40
Cathedral School of St. Mary: *see* St. Mary's School
Cathedral School of St. Paul: *see* St. Paul's School
Central Railroad of Long Island, v, viii, 8, 11, 13, 14, 30, 32, 33, 45, 56
Cherry Valley Golf Club, 38, 54, 61
Childs, George W., 29
Claydon, Bell and Co., 25
Clinch, Charles, 27, 31
Clinch, Cornelia Mitchell: *see* Stewart, Cornelia Clinch
Clinton Road Station, 63
Country Life Press, 20, 66
Country Life Press Station, 66
Curtiss, Glenn Hammond, 50, 51, 56, 76
Curtiss Aeroplane and Motor Corp., 51, 76
Curtiss Engineering Co., viii, 76
Curtiss Field: *see* Hazelhurst Field
Curtiss/Roosevelt Field: *see* Hazelhurst Field

Denton, Daniel, v, 5
Denton, Delamater, 9
"Disciple" houses, 14, 16
Doubleday, Frank Nelson, 66, 69
Doubleday, Page and Co., viii, 20, 66, 69
Dwight, Timothy, 5

Eisenhower Park, 39, 63
Embury, Aymar, 49
Emmet, Devereux, 31
Ernst, Christian, 64
Esselte Pendaflex Corp., 76
Estate Building, 14, 40, 45, 63
Evarts, Allen, 31

Floyd, Nicholl, Jr., 39
Flynn, Father James, 69
Ford, Butler and Oliver (architects), 69
Franklin Avenue, viii, 11, 45, 69
Franklin Court, 69
Franklin Court West, 20
Fuller, Dudley B., 39

Garden City Bank, 19
Garden City Casino, 37, 45
Garden City Company, v, viii, 31, 33, 34, 37, 38, 39, 43, 47, 48, 50, 53, 54, 55, 56, 63, 69
Garden City Company Office, 63
Garden City Country Club, 59, 61
Garden City East, viii, 63, 66, 69, 79
Garden City Estates, viii, 53, 55, 56, 59, 61, 79
Garden City Estates Clubhouse, 59
Garden City Estates Station, 56
Garden City Firehouse, 53, 79
Garden City Garage, 47, 48
Garden City Golf Club, 38, 40
Garden City Grammar School, 19, 20, 53
Garden City Gun Club, 39
Garden City Historical Society, 14, 29
Garden City Hotel, v, viii, 6, 11, 13, 21, 30, 32, 34, 35, 40, 42, 45, 46, 47, 48, 72
Garden City Station, v, 6, 13, 19, 37, 40, 45
Garden City Tollhouse, 63, 64
Garden City Waterworks, v, 21, 30, 32, 45
Garden City West, viii, 79
Gerard, James W., Jr., 29
"Gold Bug": *see* Golden Flyer
Gold Bug Hotel, 50
Golden Flyer, 50, 51
Grand Union Hotel (Saratoga), 2, 11, 23
"Great Iron Store," 2, 6
Grotzki (barber), 19

Harris, E. H., 27, 29
Harrison, Henry G., 25
Hazelhurst Field, viii, 61, 64, 70, 72, 73, 76, 78
Heaton, Butler and Boyne, 27
Helck, Peter, 49
Hempstead, Town of, v, 5
Hempstead Branch line: *see* Long Island Railroad
Hempstead Plains, v, 4, 5, 6, 8
Hempstead Plains Aerodrome: *see* Hazelhurst Field
Hempstead Plains Aviation Corp., 70
Hempstead Plains Company, 31
Hering, Oswald, 56
Hicks, Frederick, 45
Hilton, Judge Henry, 10, 21, 23, 27, 29, 31
Hinsdale, W. R., 14

Hitchcock, Frank H., 61
Hofstra University, viii
Hubbell, George Loring, 19, 37, 38, 40, 42, 53, 79
Hubbell's Pond, 40
Hughes, George and Gerard, 48, 73
Hunt, Richard Howland, 38, 39

International Aviation Meet, 61
Island Golf Links, 38

Jones, William, 45

Kellum, John, v, 2, 4, 6, 9, 11, 14, 16
Kirby, Petit & Green [Kirby and Petit] (architects), 55, 66
Klipp, J. F., 69

Lake Cornelia, 40
Leavitt, Charles, Jr., 55, 63
L'Hommedieu, James H., 10, 11, 14, 16, 19, 21, 25, 27, 29
Littlejohn, Bishop Abram N., 23, 25, 27, 29
"Little School," 19, 53
Long Island Motor Parkway, viii, 13, 48, 63, 64
Long Island Motor Parkway Office, 64
Long Island Railroad, v, viii, 8, 13, 30, 33, 37, 40, 43, 49, 59, 66

Mansart, François, 6
"Marble Palace," 2, 4, 6
Marchant, Edward Dalton, 23
Marshall, Cyril E., 55, 59, 63
Marshall, Ernest, 59
McKim, Mead & White, v, 34, 45
McManus, Rev. Edward, 69
Meadow Brook Hunt Club, 33, 34
Merillon Company, 31
Messereau, Willis, 19
Midland Golf Club, 38, 54
Mineola Branch line: *see* Long Island Railroad
Mineola Field: *see* Washington Avenue Field
Mitchel Field, 73, 78
Moisant, Alfred, 70
Moisant, Miss (aviator), 51

Nassau Boulevard, 56
Nassau Boulevard Aerodrome, 61
Nassau Collegiate Junior College Center, 76
Nassau County Court House, v, 33, 43, 45
NC-4 hydroplane, 51, 76
New York Aero Club: *see* New York Aeronautic Society
New York Aeronautic Society, 50, 61, 70

Osborne, Frank Sayre, 31
Ovington, Earle, 61

Page, Walter Hines, 66
Pardington, A. R., 64
Peters, Ralph, 49
Petit, A. R., 56
Pickering, William, 49
Poole's general store, 13, 19, 53
Pope, John Russell, 64
Post Office, 13, 19, 69

Queens County Fairgrounds, 32, 33, 51
Quimby, Harriet, 70

R-34 dirigible, 78
Raiche, Bessie, 51
Rainbow Division, viii, 74
Robertson, George, 49
Roosevelt, Elliott, 33
Roosevelt, Quentin, 72, 73
Roosevelt, Theodore, 43, 45, 66, 73
Roosevelt Field: *see* Hazelhurst Field
Roosevelt Shopping Center, 72
Rossiter, T. P., 2
Russell, Horace, 31

St. Joseph's Church, 69
St. Mary's School, 29
St. Paul's School, 10, 25, 27, 29
Salisbury Links: *see* Cherry Valley Golf Club
Scott, Miss (aviator), 51
Scott, Thomas, 19
Scudder, Townsend, 45
Sloane (aviator), 70
Smith, Bessie, 34
Smith, James Clinch, 31
Smith, Judge Lawrence, 34
Sperry Gyroscope Co., 76
Stable and Carriage House, v, 6, 11, 13, 40, 53, 79
Stable-Garage, 59
Stewart, Alexander Turney, v, viii, 1, 2, 4, 6, 8, 10, 11, 16, 27
Stewart, Cornelia Clinch, v, 1, 2, 4, 10, 21, 23, 27, 29, 30, 31, 34, 40
Stewart Arms (inn), 37, 69
Stewart Avenue, viii, 61, 63, 69
Subdivision East: *see* Garden City East
Sunset Division, 75

Tarbell, Gage E., 55, 56, 61, 63
Taft, Mrs. (schoolteacher), 53
Totten, Bert, 40

Travis, Walter J., 38, 54, 61
Tubby, William, 43
Turner, Lieut. William Bradford, 75
Twombly, W. Irving, 70

Unitarian Church, 56

Vanderbilt, William K., Jr., viii, 47, 48, 49, 63, 64
Vanderbilt Court, 64
Vanderbilt Cup Races, viii, 47, 48, 49, 64
Van DeWater, John, 11
Velcor, Ruth, 6
Village Hall: *see* Stable and Carriage House

Wanamaker's department stores, 2
Washington Avenue Field, 50, 51, 61
White, Stanford, 31, 34, 37
Willets, Edwin, 45
Woodruff, Timothy L., 55, 61
World War I, viii, 72, 73, 74, 75, 76, 78

Youngs, Col. William, 45